Smokin' Willie's
Guide to Great Grillin'

Smokin' Willie's
Guide to Great Grillin'
The best family recipes in the known universe!

Insider tips on sauces, spice rubs, and music to listen to while you're cookin'

Bill Kelley

Home by the Sea Press

Smokin' Willie's Guide to Great Grillin'

Copyright ©2009 William Kelley

All rights reserved. No part of this publication may be reproduced, stored in or introduced into a retrieval system, or transmitted, in any form, or by any means (electronic, mechanical, photocopying, recording or otherwise), without the prior written permission of both the copyright owner and the publisher of this book. The scanning, uploading and distribution of this book via the internet or via any other means without the written permission of the publisher is illegal and punishable by law. Please purchase only authorized electronic editions.

Home By The Sea Press
19431 Business Center Dr, Suite 34
Northridge, CA 91324
www.homebytheseapress.com
(818) 993-3463

ISBN-13: 978-0-615-23303-1
Library of Congress Control Number: 2008941948

Publisher's Cataloging-In-Publication

Kelley, Bill.

    Smokin' Willie's guide to great grillin' : the best family recipes in the known universe! : insider tips on sauces, spice rubs, and music to listen to while you're cookin' / Bill Kelley. -- 1st ed. -- Northridge, CA: Home By The Sea Press, c2009.

    p. ; cm.

    ISBN: 978- 0- 615- 23303- 1

    1. Barbecue cookery. 2. Barbecue cookery--Songs and music. 3. Dinners and dining. I. Title. II. Title: Guide to great grilling.

TX840.B3 K45 2009   2008941948
641.5/784-- dc22   2009

Cover Design & Book Design: **Bicna Bagheri**

Photography: **Jon Edwards and Associates**

Food Styling: **Denise Vivaldo**

Editors: **Larry Butler and Pamela Guerrieri**

Copywriter: **Laren Bright**

Book Consultant: **Ellen Reid**

To learn more about Bill Kelley and Smokin' Willie's Guide to Great Grillin', please visit www.smokinwillies.com.

For information regarding special sales discounts for bulk purchases as premiums or special editions, including customized covers, please contact Home by the Sea Press (818) 993-3463.

First Edition

Printed in the United States of America
10 9 8 7 6 5 4 3 2 1

Dedication

I dedicate this cookbook to the three most important women in my life:

My wife Diana, my best friend, lover, support, mother of our two sons, Matt and Nick. You make me the man that I am and you have been the source of my strength and love. I feel like the luckiest man in the world. I love you!

Mom, Diane Kelley—who taught me how to live, love, and cook. This book is really about you. Thank you for sharing your knowledge and recipes with everyone. Thank you!

Cruz Alonzo, my other mother. She gave me Diana. Cruz always fed me when I was dating Diana. It's true—a way to a man's (or woman's) heart is through good food. We miss you and may God look after your beautiful soul. Gracias!

In Memory

Rudy Hill

The first person to call me Smokin' Willie.

Smokin' Willie's Awards

2009 Fiery Foods & BBQ Show
Grilling Sauces Category (Cook-off)
1st Place Smokin' Willie's Classic BBQ Sauce
All Natural Sauces Category
3rd Place Smokin' Willie's Classic BBQ Sauce
Low Sodium Spice Rubs Category
3rd Place Smokin' Willie's BBQ Spice Rub

2008 Fiery Foods & BBQ Show
Grilling Sauces Category (Cook-off)
1st Place Smokin' Willie's Classic BBQ Sauce
2nd Place Shanghai Style BBQ Sauce
3rd Place Fiesta with Chipotle BBQ Sauce
World Sauces Category
2nd Place Shanghai Style BBQ Sauce

2007 Fiery Foods & BBQ Show
1st Place Shanghai Style BBQ Sauce
1st Place Smokin' Willie's Spice Rub
3rd Place Fiesta with Chipotle BBQ Sauce
3rd Place Shanghai Style BBQ Sauce

2007 Fiery Food Challenge (Chili Pepper Magazine)
1st Place Shanghai Style BBQ Sauce
3rd Place Smokin' Willie's Classic BBQ Sauce
3rd Place New Mexico Spice Dry Rub
3rd Place Shanghai Style BBQ Sauce

2006 America's Best Professional Food Show
1st Place Shanghai Style BBQ Sauce
2nd Place Smokin' Willie's Classic BBQ Sauce
3rd Place Smokin' Willie's Classic BBQ Sauce

2006 Fiery Foods & BBQ Show
2nd Place Fiesta with Chipotle BBQ Sauce

Acknowledgments and Gratitude

This book is only possible because of the passionate work and support of so many people. I want to thank everyone who worked so hard to create this book that I have dreamed about for so long:

Ellen Reid, my Book Shepherd, who guided me to make my dream become a reality. Bicna Bagheri, you exceeded my vision for the design of this book. Jon Edwards, your amazing pictures speak volumes. Denise Vivaldo, you brought the food to life. Larry Butler and Pamela Guerrieri, thank God for editors. Laren Bright, your words are inspirational. Craig Landers, Kim Hawley, and everyone at Taylor Specialty Books.

Michael Acuña, who developed the Smokin' Willie's line of award-winning BBQ sauces and spice rubs into a class act! There would not be a Smokin' Willie's without you. Bicna and Frank Bagheri, you have been there from the onset. Your vision and support have been priceless to me. Alisse Kingsley, who helped me with publicity, support, and friendship. I could not have done it without you! And Rachel too.

Everyone at Pacifica Foods, Ken, Mark, Joe, Kim, and Tina. Steve Brown, you gave me my first big break, thank you! Richie Beaulieu, Michael Overing, Nancy Brown, Derek Harrison, Charlie Cox, George Denue, Mike Kennedy, Mike McMahon, Gary Christansen, and Harold Smith.

I want to thank my family and friends who have supported me in the evolution of Smokin' Willie's! Diana, I love you. Matt and Nick, our sons' love and support have helped me through the tough times and made the good times great. Mom, where would I be without you? Dad, "Wish You Were Here." My brothers and sisters, Bill DuMong, Douglas and Carrie Wong, Ken LeMunion, Dean LaValley, Joe Teurlings, and the countless others, too many to name, that have stood behind me all the way!

Thank you.

Contents

grillin' 101 / you can grill!

- 1   A Personal Greeting from Smokin' Willie
- 2   The Story of Smokin' Willie's
- 4   Please Read First
- 5   Smokin' Willie's Grillin' Tips

appetizers

- 10   Bacon-Wrapped Scallops
- 12   BBQ Stuffed Shiitake Mushrooms
- 14   Diana's BBQ Hot Wings and Dip
- 15   Grilled Salsa
- 16   Guida's Quesadillas
- 18   Shanghai Chicken Lettuce Wraps
- 20   Asian Meatball Hors d'oeuvres
- 22   Shanghai Shrimp on a Stick

side dishes

- 25   BBQ Chicken Salad
- 26   Bicna's BBQ Pork Salad
- 27   Michael's Potato Salad
- 28   Mom's BBQ Baked Beans
- 30   Southwestern Wild Rice Stuffing
- 31   Twin's Corn Bread
- 32   Mom's Quick Corn Bread
- 34   Grilled Veggies
- 36   BBQ Potatoes
- 37   Grilled Baked Potatoes and Yams
- 38   Grilled Asparagus
- 39   Grilled Corn on the Cob
- 40   Smokin' Corn for a Crew
- 42   Grilled Garlic and Garlic Bread Spread
- 43   Grilled Mushrooms and Portobello & Fresh Cheese Sandwich
- 44   Grilled Onions
- 45   Grilled Peppers
- 46   Mixed Veggies

sandwiches

- 48   Pulled Pork
- 50   BBQ Meatball Sandwich
- 52   Mary and Mason's Grilled Cheese Sandwich
- 53   Southwestern Spicy Chicken Burger
- 54   Shanghai Turkey Burger
- 56   Teriyaki Sandwich

Contents

main dishes

58	T-Bone & Porterhouse Steak
60	Smokin' Willie's Ribs
62	Smokin' Willie's Chicken
64	Award-Winning Tri-Tip
66	Ahi Tuna Shanghai Style
68	BBQ Red Snapper
70	Cruz's Kabobs
72	Smokin' Fajitas
74	Devin's Kielbasa
75	Dad's Steak
76	Shanghai Chicken on a Stick
77	Asian Chicken Kabobs
78	Matt's Grilled Tofu
80	Smokin' Willie's Meatloaf

group fixin's

82	Camping
83	Breakfast Burritos
84	Dad's Camping Chicken
86	Mom's Crew Q
88	Smokin' Willie's BBQ Turkey

marinades, sauces, and butters

90	Smokin' Fowl Soak for BBQ Turkey
91	BBQ Soak
92	Basil Garlic Mayonnaise
93	Fiesta Seafood Cocktail Sauce
94	Grillin' Butters
95	Flavored Butters
96	Grilled Vegetable Spread/Dip
97	Veggie Marinades

desserts

99	Grilled Fruit
100	Bill's Grilled Bananas
101	Grilled Pears
102	Fruit Kabobs
104	Nick's Stuffed Apples and Pears
106	Bonus Recipe! Gram's Chocolate-Lovers Cake

The Overland trip of the William Rogers Trains to California.

We shall first mention in Chronological order the several trains in which the various members of the William Rogers family crossed the Plains by the Sante Fe trail from Texas.

In 1856 Frank Foley (who afterward married Alcie Rogers) made the trip with several other members and their families. 1865 was the year in which J.H. Allen and his wife Mildred Rogers Allen with their four daughters and one son came across the plains with quite a large train.

In 1869 a number of families including S.D. White, his wife Nancy Rogers White and their two sons Lee and Lewis, made the journey overland from Texas.

Grandfather William Rogers started out for California over the Sante Fe trail with ox teams from a place near McKinney, Collin Co. Texas in May, 1868. Travelling with him were his

A page from an original wagon train journal that my great-grandfather wrote.

A Personal Greeting from Smokin' Willie

This book is about family—personal family recipes, stories, and history. Some of my fondest memories revolve around family gatherings, music, and food. As my Aunt "Tia" Vera says, "Cook with lots of love in your heart and your food will always turn out great." I believe the truth of this statement, and I try to cook with the same passion Tia Vera applied to her magic in the kitchen. It doesn't hurt that I like to eat with love and passion as well!

I like to think of a family meal as a work of art. Some meals are ornate masterpieces while others are a simple watercolor. These works of art are momentary, only lasting as long as the meal. Yet the smell, color, texture, and taste all offer a wonderful palette for the palate. Each meal is unique and delightful in its own way. I have savored Mom's big holiday masterpieces, but I can also remember a hearty bowl of soup and a grilled cheese sandwich after coming in from the cold. Like different tastes in art and music, there are countless tastes in food, and it is up to you as the artist to craft your own masterpieces for your family and friends.

I fear that "the art of the family meal" is dying in these fast-paced times. When I was growing up, my mom would usher our family into the dining room to eat as many of our meals together as possible, and dinner was almost always a "Family Affair." Families joining at the same table at the same time for a meal seems to be the exception, not the rule, in these hectic and busy times. But meals should offer important quality time together to find out how everyone's day is going, how we are feeling; it's an opportunity to talk, laugh, and sometimes cry.

One of my favorite mealtimes is when we're outside, grilling to some energizing tunes. A barbecue is a fun and fulfilling way to celebrate family meals, and even teenagers will stay for a good "Q." It is my hope that more people will eat together as a family and practice cooking as an art!

My goal in writing this book is to show how much fun and how easy grilling can be. Don't be afraid to try new recipes and grill different types of food.

And guys, watch out—women are the fastest growing group of grillers! Many recipes can be cooked on the stove top or in the oven when the weather does not cooperate. Enjoy yourself, listen to music, and use these recipes to create your own works of art so that you can become the "BBQ Champion/Grill Master" of your family and neighborhood.

Keep on Grillin'!

The Story of Smokin' Willie's

It all began with Mom in 1967. We lived in Lakeview Terrace, California, a suburb of Los Angeles. It was early on a Saturday morning when an old pick-up truck with a homemade fifty-five gallon barrel BBQ on a trailer (both of which looked like they had seen better days) pulled up across the street. As cars lined our street and children and adults poured onto the property, the growing chatter announced a family reunion taking place.

That afternoon they started the BBQ on the driveway, and within a couple of hours an amazing smoky aroma drifted in the direction of our house, driving us all crazy. As soon as Mom's nose got a whiff of what they were barbequing, she invited herself to their family reunion and later came back raving about the BBQ—particularly the sauce that they used. Mom begged for the BBQ sauce recipe, but to no avail. She was unable to finagle the recipe out of them.

Finally, after what seemed like endless intense nagging and maybe even some threats (desperate people do crazy things) Mom got a list of most of the ingredients on a paper napkin. With this dream recipe clutched in her hands, she practically ran home to make the first batch of sauce and ended up sorely disappointed. The sauce turned out bland and was definitely not the sauce she had tasted at the party.

Mom was on a quest to make this sauce work, so she started researching BBQ sauce recipes from various parts of the country—adding a little of this, taking away that, more of this and less of that. In the end Mom made countless batches of BBQ sauce, each an improvement over the previous batch—until she crafted her final product. In 1969, to celebrate the Apollo landing on the moon, we held a neighborhood barbecue and Mom's sauce was a hit. Man landed on the moon, and Mom ventured to bold new territories. Smokin' Willie's BBQ Sauce was established!

With taste test approval, Mom started canning the sauce in mason jars and demand grew. In the early 1990s, she was making and selling the sauce to help sponsor my brother Brian's race car. Mom had been a stock car race fan for as long as I can remember, and she is Brian's number one fan to this day.

While Mom's sauce continued to be a hit, I was working for Warner Bros. Records and had the best job in the world! Yet as the music industry became more corporate, money became more important than the quality of the music and I started looking into other endeavors for the future. The demand for Mom's sauce was increasing, so I began to help her mix larger batches.

And then the ideas started exploding into new ventures.

One day Mom said that she wished she could share "the best BBQ sauce" with more people. So in 1999 I started Wild Bill's Foods—an attempt to try and market Mom's sauce. After a few tries, none very successful, I shelved the BBQ sauce pitch to make a living in the banking industry. Eventually I was missing the sauce and Mom was missing me!

Bored by the financial world but having socked away some cash, on February 22, 2005, Smokin' Willie's was reborn. Veteran Chef Michael Acuna was brought on board and, with his amazing talent, he turned Mom's recipe into an award-winning manufacturing formula. When we brought Mom to the manufacturing plant for the first run, she tasted the sauce and with a tear in her eye she said, "You did it. Now I don't have to cook the sauce for six hours anymore." And with Mom's blessing, we were off and running.

Please Read First

I will be suggesting Smokin' Willie's brand of award-winning BBQ sauces and spice rubs in most of the recipes in this book. Of course, I am a little biased because this is my sauce! The Classic BBQ Sauce used for many recipes is my mom's original homemade recipe that I have been enjoying since the 1960s (I am still not tired of it). You can use your favorite brand or homemade BBQ sauce instead, but I hope you will consider trying Smokin' Willie's Grilling Sauces and Spice Rubs to achieve the full flavor of each recipe.

With a little time and practice, soon you will be the grill master of your home. Though remember—"it is all a matter of taste!"

I do not use measurements for basic ingredients like salt and pepper, because different people prefer different amounts in their food. I personally add a little salt at a time while tasting as I go because I want to enhance the flavor of the food but I do not like anything to taste too salty. I use kosher or sea salt in my kitchen, and I prefer freshly ground pepper from a pepper mill.

Eighty percent of grillers use gas grills, so most of the recipes are for use with a gas grill. I personally use a charcoal grill at home and have made all of these recipes using charcoal, and many of them using an electric or a gas grill. You can use any grilling method accessible to you and still get great results. You will be surprised at how tasty most of these recipes are when they are cooked in the oven, on a stove top, and in slow cookers.

A favorite feature of grillin' for me includes the atmosphere, along with the food. As a lover of music, it has always been a part of my life. With each recipe I include my personal Listening Suggestions—songs that I often listen to while prepping, cooking, grilling, and eating. Listed are many of my favorite songs, including songs with titles or artists that remind me of the recipe. Many years in the music industry have given me quite a diverse library of music, with some well-known songs and other more obscure songs. People's taste in music is as diverse as their taste in food, so I have tried to suggest songs that are just as varied. Build your own "playlists" for you to enjoy while you grill!

Finally, experiment with these recipes; nothing would please me more than for you to take any of these recipes and make them your own creation by trying different flavors and ingredients.

Spread the word … If you like this book, recipes, sauces, and spice rubs, please tell your family and friends!

Thank you.

Smokin' Willie's Grillin' Tips

The one rule in grilling is that there are no rules. There are as many ways to grill as there are people. I grill food to taste the way I like to eat, and so should you.

Grilling requires no complex recipes, no special cooking-school techniques.

Everybody can be a grillin' expert in a very short time with some simple tricks of the trade. The more you grill, the better you will get. Don't worry about making a few mistakes along the way. Here's the first trick to know: Always have as backup a pack of quality hot dogs or kielbasa. It's a quick and surefire cure for when something accidentally goes up in flames.

This book contains my very favorite recipes from over thirty years of grillin'. Keep in mind that you do not have to slavishly follow these. Add ingredients, make quantities larger (or smaller), and by all means, experiment and make the recipes your own. That's what grillin' is all about!

Now before you get started, let me share with you some nuggets of wisdom that I've picked up along the way:

Smokin' Willie's Helpful Grillin' Tips

1. **Have Fun!** If you're stressed while grillin', you're taking it way too seriously. (To liven the atmosphere, I suggest playing your favorite music while you grill.)

2. **Don't Be Afraid of Flavor.** As a rule, more is better. You gotta taste the darn thing you are grillin'. You can become the backyard champ with Smokin' Willie's, so pack on the rubs and slather on the sauce.

3. **Safety Always First.** The goal is to enjoy yourself, but never at the expense of safety. After all, we're talking about heat from a fire that's at the heart of grillin', so as you might guess, burns are among the most prevalent injuries. And because we're also working with very sharp objects, cuts come in a close second. But here's something you might not think about—bacteria. Grillin' does not automatically kill all germs. Handling food safely prior to cooking is very important, so keep your friends and loved ones safe by keeping a) your hands and utensils clean, and b) your raw foods refrigerated and separate from cooked foods. Please, do not use canned cooking oil sprays, like Pam® on a hot grate. This can cause the spray to flame up and can cause serious burns. The instruction on the cans have "DO NOT SPRAY INTO OPEN FLAMES" in bold letters. A much safer way is to put some olive oil on a paper towel and use your tongs to oil the grates. Please do not do this over flames.

4. **Prepare Ahead of Time.** That might seem like a no-brainer, but spending just a little a bit of time prepping your food before it hits the grill is the best way to ensure success every time. Prepping your "Q" will make it easier, tastier, and more enjoyable!

5. **Keep Forks at Bay.** Use tongs or a spatula when grillin'. Forks pierce the foods, allowing the juices to run out, and the flavor and tenderness along with them.

6. **Give It a Rest.** Let your grilled meat rest before cutting. You see, when you cook meat, the molecular cells constrict, forcing the juices out. When you let meat rest, most of the juices

are absorbed back into the cells. Science lesson now over!

7. **Use Direct and Indirect Heat**. This is a simple but often overlooked rule. You want two kinds of heat at play to grill successfully—direct and indirect. Direct heat means you are cooking directly over the heat source (charcoal or the flames from the burners) and that you have enough heat to sear the food. Once you sear over the direct heat, you finish the cooking process and brush on the BBQ sauce over indirect heat. To create this effect on your gas BBQ, you warm up the grill by turning all of the burners on for 5 to 10 minutes and then turn half of the burners off on one side just before you start to cook. With a charcoal BBQ, I start the coals in a charcoal chimney starter; they are like a large can with a handle and you use newspaper to start the charcoal. I do not use starter fluid because of the taste it adds to the food and it can be dangerous. After the coals are ready, about 15 to 20 minutes, I place the hot coals on one half of the bottom the BBQ and leave the other side bare. When you are searing the meat over the direct heat and you get a flare-up, just move the meat over the indirect part of the grill and close the lid until the flame dies down. You can then finish searing.

8. **No Overcrowding**. There's no way to properly sear if your grill is piled high with meat. It simply doesn't allow enough room to sear properly. Unless you have a very large grill, only put a few pieces on at a time and keep the rest warm. Grillin' is generally fast, so no one will go hungry for long.

9. **BBQ Soak**. This is grillin' lingo for brining or marinating. A "soak" acts to tenderize the meat and add flavor. I soak my ribs, chicken (with skin on), and pork. I do not soak fish because it tends to fall apart.

10. **Slow and Low.** For larger cuts of meat or ribs, sear over high heat to create a crust and seal in the important juices, then move the meat over indirect heat. Try to keep from opening the lid of the BBQ too often because every time you lift the lid, you lose heat and this extends the cooking time. You do not have to worry about flare-ups because the meat is not directly over the flame.

11. **Pull Membranes Back**. When you're grillin' ribs, first pull the membrane from the back of the ribs. Sear the top of the ribs first, and then cook the bottom slower and longer. (See the rib recipe on page 60 for more details.)

12. **Timing**. As they say in the music business, "Timing is everything." Well, timing is just as important when it comes to grilling. There are several variables that can affect your timing—heat of the grill, thickness of the meat, the type of meat, lifting the lid too much, running out of propane, the weather, or even getting distracted and forgetting about what is cooking on the grill! There are estimated grilling times given in this book, but you will have to take into account all of these different variables when you are the grill master of your domain. One of the questions that I am asked frequently is, "Why is the outside burned and the inside raw?" To prevent a charred exterior, wait until the last 10 to 15 minutes of grilling time to brush on any BBQ sauce that you are using, and do this over indirect heat to keep from burning the sauce. If you are just starting out grilling or in doubt, use a thermometer to check the inside of the meat to make sure it is cooked properly. Check the temperature chart on page 8 for the correct cooking temperatures.

13. **Grill, BBQ, or Smoking?** Grilling is the term used to describe the quickest way of cooking on a barbecue. Usually one hour or less using direct/indirect heat. Barbequing is the term used for slower cooking; an hour or more using mostly indirect heat. Smokin', as you might guess, is even slower since it uses low, indirect heat and smoke from wood or wood chips. Count on several hours for this cooking method.

14. **Wood Chips and Chunks.** There are many different types of wood used in wood chunks and chips for the grill to add smoky flavor to your "Q." Hickory, apple, mesquite, cherry, grapevines—even wood from barrels used in making Jack Daniel's whiskey! These wood chips can be purchased in any store that sells barbecues, hardware stores, some grocery stores, and of course online. Use wood chips and pellets with a gas BBQ and wood chunks with charcoal. I soak 2 or 3 chunks of wood for charcoal or about a cup full of wood chips in water at least 30 minutes before I start the grill. I add these soaked wood chips at the beginning, directly on 1 or 2 coals or in a container just for that purpose just before I first put the meat on the grill. The goal is to have the wood slowly smolder and smoke, not to burn up in flames. I want the smoky flavor to start flavoring the meat right away. The smoke from the flavored wood chips gives your "Q" an added flavor bonus and the smell will set your salivary glands drooling. Some people do not think it is worth the effort, but I use them quite a bit with ribs, chicken, Tri-Tip, roasts, Mom's crew "Q," or recipes that are cooked on the grill for longer periods of time. Try it; I hope you like it!

15. **Gas, Charcoal, Electric, Wood BBQs, Oven, or on the Stove**.

Gas Grills: I have used and like gas BBQs. They are easy to keep clean and you do not have to empty the ashes. This is the easiest BBQ to control the heat. Just make sure you have plenty of propane on hand to finish cooking your meal. There's nothing worse than making a run to get propane while in the middle of grilling a meal. Some people have both gas and charcoal grills just for that reason!

Charcoal Grills: I have always owned and used a charcoal grill, so I am a charcoal and wood chunks griller. I like the extra flavor that charcoal and wood chunks add to my dishes. Here are some of the different types of charcoal grills: charcoal BBQ, hibachi, kettle grill, 55-gallon drum, brick, and stone grills.

Electric: There are many electric grills on the market today, from the tabletop George Foreman Grills to expensive stand-alone models. I would use thinner foods with the electric grill, such as hamburgers, hot dogs, sausages, boneless and skinless chicken breasts, kabobs, thin steaks, and pork chops. (I think you get the idea—nothing that is too thick or takes a long time to cook.)

Wood: Wood is used for smoking and barbequing for long periods of time. I have used wood rarely, but when I do, it is for camping, smoking, or if I am going to BBQ a big piece of meat on the grill for an extended amount of time.

Oven: You can bake many of these recipes in the oven. When I use the oven, I put the rubs and the BBQ sauce on before I put the food in the oven. The smell of BBQ in your kitchen will drive everyone to the dinner table!

Stove Top: Skillet grills, or even a basic frying pan, can be used on the stove in a pinch, like when it is raining and you have a craving for that BBQ flavor.

16. **BBQ Grates**. I recommend cast iron cooking grates for your BBQ. They usually come standard with stainless steel grates. I use cast iron grates because they retain the heat better (just like Grandma's cast iron skillet), there's less chance of food falling between the grates, and you will get those "Steak House" grill marks on your food. I used cast iron grates when I grilled the food for the photos for this book and you can get the same great look for your meals. You can order cast iron grates for your BBQ from the manufacturer or shop online. I think it will be worth your time and effort.

17. **BBQ Sauces**. There are so many different types and flavors of BBQ sauces from all parts of the U.S.A and the world. Here are a few things I look for in a BBQ sauce:

Flavor: I look for a good depth of flavor that is not overly sweet that will compliment, not overpower, what I am cooking on the grill.

What is in the sauce? I try to avoid high-fructose corn syrup in any product that I am going to use on the high heat of a grill. This sweetener is used in a majority of the BBQ sauces and marinades that are available. I find that high-fructose corn syrup is overly sweet and burns or turns dark when used on the BBQ. The most frequent question that is asked at my grilling classes or demos is, "Why is the outside burned and the inside raw?" I feel that the main reason is using BBQ sauces with high-fructose corn syrup; so do not marinade the meats with anything that has sugar in it. Also, apply the BBQ sauce during the last 10 minutes on the grill, over indirect heat. Your BBQ sauce will become a nice glaze, not a burnt crust.

Try Smokin' Willie's award-winning BBQ sauces the next time you fire up the grill; they contain no high-fructose corn syrup.

18. **Spice Rubs**. The use of spice rubs on your food will help you on the path to becoming a "Grill Master." BBQ cook-off champions all have their "secret" spice rubs and BBQ sauces. The first thing the competitors do is trim the meat and apply a good coating of spice rub as soon as they can. The thick coating of seasonings and spices will create a tasty crust that coats the meat and seals in the precious juices and enhances the flavor of the meat.

As they say on TV cooking shows, "You have to season what you are cooking to enhance the flavors." I think that it is just as important on the grill, if not more. As simple as salt and pepper, homemade blends to Smokin' Willie's award-winning BBQ spice rubs, I feel that your food will taste better if you use spice rubs when you prepare your food for the grill. I will apply my spice rub the day before on beef, pork, and chicken and on seafood the same day that I am going to grill.

When it comes to grillin', I live by the Golden Rule. Grill unto others as you would have them grill unto you! By following these simple tips, you can keep it fun, delicious, and safe.

COOKING TEMPERATURE CHART

Type of Meat	Minimum Internal Cooking Temperature
Poultry	165 °F (74 °C)
Ground Meats	155 °F (68 °C)
Beef, Pork, Veal, Lamb	145 °F (63 °C)
Fish	145 °F (63 °C)

The temperatures are the minimum safe recommendation. When taking the temperature, make sure that the thermometer is not touching the bone.

Source: ServSafe class under the National Restaurant Association Education Foundation.

appetizers

BACON-WRAPPED SCALLOPS

2 to 4 scallops per person, depending on size

1 strip of bacon per scallop

Salt

Pepper

Toothpicks

Lemon, or lemon juice

Smokin' Willie's Shanghai BBQ Sauce

Slightly cook bacon; you still want the bacon flexible enough to wrap around the scallops. Drain bacon on a paper towel. This will keep you from getting flare-ups and overcooking scallops while still crisping the bacon on the grill. Rinse the scallops in a colander and pat dry with a paper towel. Lightly season scallops with salt and pepper, and wrap each one with a strip of bacon. Secure the end of the bacon with a toothpick through the center of the scallop. (I put the completed scallops on a platter and cover with Saran™ wrap, then place in the refrigerator until ready to grill, up to 2 hours in advance.)

Grill should be set to medium heat and lightly wiped with a paper towel coated in olive oil (use your tongs to wipe the grill). You will need to stand by the grill for the full cooking time with this recipe. Squeeze fresh lemon juice on scallops just before putting on the grill. Place scallops, bacon side down, on grill with the toothpicks faced downward between the grates, then roll them as the bacon crisps, 5 to 8 minutes. Lastly, turn scallops on the flat side for a few minutes, then flip. Brush a glaze of Smokin' Willie's Shanghai BBQ Sauce on the just cooked side. Turn over indirect heat and glaze the other side. Serve hot off the grill!

30 minutes preparation
10 to 15 minutes grilling

This is the surf in my Mother's Day Surf & Turf brunch recipe. What an elegant but easy dish to make, and all of the work is in the prep. This past Mother's Day I planned to prepare a meal for the beautiful moms in my life—my wife Diana, my mom, and Olivia, my sister-in-law. I was at the butcher shop buying shrimp and Châteaubriand for my Surf & Turf. As I examined the shrimp, they looked just okay, but they had some amazing fresh scallops! I bought 1 ½ pounds of scallops and ordered some freshly cut bacon. Grilled and finished off with a coating of Smokin' Willie's Shanghai BBQ Sauce, the moms were impressed by the Bacon-Wrapped Scallops.

Suggested Listening:

Love and Happiness *Al Green*
Heard It in a Love Song
 The Marshall Tucker Band
The Payback *James Brown*
How Sweet It Is (To Be Loved By You) *Marvin Gaye*
(You'll Be) Satisfied *the subdudes*
Nothing Compares 2 U *Prince*
Whipping Post
 The Allman Brothers Band
Mother and Child Reunion
 Paul Simon
Messin' With the Kid *Junior Wells*
Giant Steps *John Coltrane*

BBQ Stuffed Shiitake Mushrooms

½ pound ground pork

10-15 dried large shiitake mushrooms

1 cup chicken broth

3 tablespoons Smokin' Willie's Shanghai sauce

½ cup finely chopped green onions

1 tablespoon chopped shallots

¼ cup coarsely chopped water chestnuts

1 teaspoon fresh black pepper

Soak the mushrooms in hot water for 1 hour. Cut off all hard stems from mushrooms. Rinse and squeeze excess water, place in bowl, pour 1 cup of hot chicken broth over mushrooms, and let soak for 30 minutes. Remove the mushrooms from the broth and lightly squeeze the broth out of the mushrooms. Don't squeeze too hard; you want to leave some of the broth for flavor.

Mix together the ground pork, sauce, green onion, shallots, water chestnuts, and pepper to incorporate.

Overstuff the shiitake mushrooms with the meat mixture. Use a spoon to fill, and then round off and smooth the tops of the mushrooms.

Broil on greased cookie sheet for about 5–10 minutes until the meat is cooked and browned on top. Just before serving, put the shiitake side down on the BBQ for 5 minutes.

Use extra warm Smokin' Willie's Shanghai sauce to drizzle over the top of the mushrooms.

If you want soup to accompany this appetizer, bring chicken broth to a soft boil, gently place the stuffed mushrooms in the broth, and cook for 15 minutes. Serve hot with chopped cilantro and green onions sprinkled atop the soup when you serve.

1½ hours soaking time
20 minutes prep time
15 to 30 minutes cooking time

This recipe is one shared by Bicna Bagheri, a close friend and fan of the sauces and rubs, and who just so happens to be my graphic designer. When I tried these BBQ stuffed mushrooms I was blown away by the great textures and flavors, and she used the Shanghai BBQ Sauce to boot. I am including Bicna's story about how this recipe has evolved to show you that you can modify almost any recipe and make it your own!

"My kind and gentle mother was an excellent cook who inspired this recipe. She used to make pork stuffed shiitake soup that I loved so much. Vietnamese meals always include a soup, and growing up my father used to remind me that it's not a complete dinner without a soup. I was the family's cook with my father's help at the age of 13, when our beloved mother died of cancer. Our typical dinner consists of a hot pot of steamed rice; a clear broth soup with stuffed shiitake, tofu, and/or veggies; a steamed veggie dish such as Vietnamese water spinach (rau muon) or green beans with tomatoes; and a fish/meat dish. As children we served our parents the bowls of rice first, and then ourselves; then with chopsticks we selected different dishes to eat together with the rice. The soups can also be spooned over the rice. I've re-invented this stuffed shiitake as a wonderful grilled appetizer."

Listening Suggestions:
Bicna's mother was a classical pianist, and her favorites were Beethoven and Bach. Bicna's favorite classical is Gershwin.

Also recommended are:
Only Mama Knows *Paul McCartney*
Tears In Heaven *Joshua Redman*
Shining Star *Earth, Wind & Fire*
Ko-Ko *Charlie Parker*
Twisting By the Pool *Dire Straits*
The Feeling *Albert King*
Chain of Fools *Aretha Franklin*
Stay With Me *The Faces*
You're the Inspiration *Chicago*
Loves Me Like a Rock *Paul Simon*

Diana's BBQ Hot Wings and Dip

2 to 3 pounds cut up chicken wings (thawed if frozen)

Smokin' Willie's New Mexico Spice Rub

Smokin' Willie's Fiesta with Chipotle BBQ Sauce

Wash chicken wings in warm water. Drain in colander. Coat wings with Spice Rub to taste; this should be done just prior to grilling. Grill wings over medium high heat 5 to 10 minutes and then turn over and grill for another 5 to 10 minutes to get a good roasted color. Move over indirect heat and brush on Smokin' Willie's Fiesta with Chipotle BBQ Sauce. Close lid and let sauce glaze on the wings for about 5 to 10 minutes. You can serve them right off the grill.

Bake in a foil tray/roasting pan or put them in a slow cooker/Crock-Pot for gatherings, parties, or the big game!

Options: Use Smokin' Willie's Classic BBQ Sauce for a milder BBQ flavor. Use Smokin' Willie's Shanghai BBQ Sauce for an amazing Asian twist; grill asparagus and serve with white or brown rice. You can heat up Shanghai sauce in the microwave or on the stove top to use as a dipping sauce.

Hot Wings Dip

¼ cup ranch salad dressing, blue cheese salad dressing, or sour cream

¼ cup Smokin' Willie's Fiesta with Chipotle BBQ Sauce

Add hot sauce to taste and bring up the heat!

Mix well in a bowl and refrigerate. This sauce makes a great sandwich spread or veggie dip as well as a tasty wing dip.

Option: Use Smokin' Willie's Classic BBQ Sauce for a milder dip.

10 minute prep
25 minutes on the grill

My wife, Diana, loves hot wings. One day she asked me to grill some hot wings instead of frying them. They turned out amazing. If they are not hot enough for your taste, you can make them as spicy as you like by simply adding some of your favorite hot sauce … and there is always someone who wants them hotter. If you like things spicy, you should attend the Fiery Food & BBQ Show in Albuquerque, New Mexico, to see how hot sauces can get and how many different kinds are out there. Diana will sometimes add Crystal Hot Sauce or Tabasco when she wants an extra kick! Use the Hot Wing Dip for a tasty alternative to blue cheese or ranch dressing.

Suggested Listening:

Hot Stuff *Rod Stewart*
Hot, Hot, Hot *Arrow*
Little Wing *Jimi Hendrix*
Wonderful Tonight *Eric Clapton*
How Much for Your Wings
  The Black Crows
The Girl from Impanema
  Antonio Carlos Jobin
You Really Got Me *The Kinks*
This Is How We Do It *Montell Jordan*
Hot Blooded *Foreigner*
Once Bitten Twice Shy
  Ian Hunter with Mick Ronson

Grilled Salsa

2 jalapeno chiles (or use your favorite chiles)

1 pasilla chile

1 large brown onion (red is also tasty)

3 large tomatoes

6 large garlic cloves

Juice of 2 limes or 1 lemon

Salt

Pepper

Cilantro

Wash chiles and tomatoes. Pierce ends of the chiles with a toothpick or knife. Remove the skin from the garlic and onion and slice onion into thick round slices. Place garlic cloves, onion slices, whole or halved tomatoes, and chiles on grill at high heat. Sear for about 10 to 20 minutes to soften and absorb the smoky flavor and to char the skin of the chiles and tomatoes. Remove from grill and place on a plate or bowl and let cool to room temperature.

Place garlic, chiles, and onions along with salt, pepper, lime juice, and cilantro in a food processor or blender and purée. Then place the rest of the cooked ingredients into the blender to break everything up. I like to make it chunky, but you can keep pulsing until you get to the consistency that you like. Refrigerate for at least one hour or more; it tastes better chilled. Before serving this tasty salsa, you can add a garnish of cilantro and grilled corn, or chunks of avocado for additional flavor and texture. Store any leftover salsa in the refrigerator for up to 2 or 3 days, but this salsa is so good it will be gone long before then.

Important addition to: fajitas, quesadillas, breakfast burritos, smokin' meatloaf, and any meal in which you want to add spice and flavor!

10 minutes prep
20 minutes grill time
10 minutes to process

This fresh salsa can be grilled to add a great smoky flavor. Sear the chiles, onion, garlic, and tomatoes and then puree in a food processor or blender with cilantro. Salt and pepper to taste and you end up with a savory salsa. You control the heat with the type and amount of chiles that you use. Removing the seeds and veins will remove some of the heat in the chiles. Here is my version, but go ahead and add or delete quantities or ingredients to better fit the tastes of you and your family and friends. You can make this salsa fresh without grilling if you prefer. I recommend that you use gloves when handling the chiles. This is dedicated to Nori and Dolores, who taught me how to make roasted salsa.

Suggested Listening:

My Friends
   The Red Hot Chili Peppers
Walk On the Wild Side *Lou Reed*
Everybody Hurts *R.E.M.*
Suffragette City *David Bowie*
Light My Fire *The Doors*
Hotter Than 'ell
   Fletcher Henderson & His Orchestra
The Gambler *Kenny Rogers*
Eruption *Van Halen*
Here Comes Those Tears Again
   Jackson Browne
This Charming Man *The Smiths*
Handle With Care
   The Traveling Wilburys

Guida's Quesadillas

1 bottle Smokin' Willie's Classic or Fiesta BBQ & Grilling Sauce

1 dozen flour tortillas

¾ to 1 pound shredded cheese (cheddar, jack, Mexican, or experiment!)

Spread BBQ sauce to taste on one side of a tortilla and then add shredded cheese and/or options. Spread BBQ sauce on second tortilla and place sauce side down on top of the cheese. Grill quesadillas until golden brown. Let the quesadillas cool for a few minutes before eating. (Caution: Cheese will be hot and they will disappear if left unattended).

Options: Use Classic BBQ Sauce for the kids or use the Fiesta with Chipotle BBQ Sauce for some added kick. Add chicken, beef, pork, or shrimp for some amazing variations!

12 to 15 minutes prep and cooking time
2 minutes to eat them!

The idea for these BBQ Quesadillas came up when my wife Diana's Primo (Cousin) Tom was on location for the film The Alamo and had been gone for about a month. Our family was invited to have a barbecue with Tom's sons and his wife Christina (whom Tom nicknamed Guida). I was cooking some Tri-Tip on the grill and had brought along the fixings' for quesadillas. I thought why not try the quesadillas with some Smokin' Willie's BBQ Sauce? I made one and put it on the counter in the kitchen to cool off. A few minutes later Christina (Guida) came out laughing, telling me that the quesadilla was gone! The boys went wild over it, so I made the rest of the quesadillas with Smokin' Willie's BBQ Sauce and everybody loved them, not just the kids. From then on we called the BBQ Quesadillas "Guida's Quesadillas."

Suggested Listening:

Papa Was a Rolling Stone
  The Temptations
More Than a Feeling *Boston*
Tequila Sunrise *The Eagles*
Living In the USA
  The Steve Miller Band
Love Her Madly *The Doors*
Here, There, and Everywhere
  The Beatles
I'll Be Around *The Spinners*
Born To Be Wild *Steppenwolf*
Take the "A" Train *Duke Ellington*
Baby Please Don't Go
  Lightnin' Hopkins

Shanghai Chicken Lettuce Wraps

1 pound ground chicken

½ cup Smokin' Willie's Shanghai BBQ Sauce or more to taste

2 green onions, finely sliced

2 tablespoons water chestnuts, finely diced

1 teaspoon toasted sesame seeds

12 lettuce leaves

Wash and dry lettuce leaves. Brown ground meat in a skillet, 7 to 10 minutes or until completely cooked and then drain any fat. Add Shanghai BBQ sauce; add more or less to taste. Pour a little from the bottle and stir meat mixture, adding more sauce until the meat is lightly coated. Add green onions and water chestnuts and sauté until steaming hot. Remove from the stove and add toasted sesame seeds just before serving. Serve this dinner right from the stove; it stays warm and we have to wash the skillet anyways.

Serving Suggestions: steamed rice or fried rice and a stir fry are one of our favorite meals.

BBQ stuffed shiitake mushrooms, BBQ pork salad, and Shanghai chicken kabobs are other options.

20 minutes prep and cook time

Here is one of my fast and easy recipes that has become one of our family favorites. I have tried different lettuce wraps in restaurants and even from the club stores and they are good, but you can do better in your own kitchen. The secret is the rich flavor of the award-winning Smokin' Willie's Shanghai BBQ Sauce. Ground chicken or turkey can be used along with many different types of lettuce to choose from. Iceberg seems to be the lettuce served most the time, but red leafy or romaine tastes great. Use your favorite. Serve the lettuce wraps with stir fry and steamed rice. You can feed a large group by preparing the chicken ahead of time and keeping it hot in a Crock-Pot, or it can be reheated in the microwave.

Suggested Listening:

Heavenly Bodies *Lee Ritenour*
Avalon *Roxy Music*
Comfortably Numb *Pink Floyd*
Lucky Star *Madonna*
Levon *Elton John*
Blinded By the Light
  Manfred Mann's Earth Band
I Was Fooled *Billy Boy Arnold*
The Jack *AC/DC*
Let's Go Crazy *Prince*
Moon Dreams *Miles Davis*
Ain't Misbehavin' *Louis Armstrong*

Asian Meatball Hors d'oeuvres

3 pounds frozen meatballs (defrosted)

1 bottle Smokin' Willie's Shanghai BBQ Sauce

2 tablespoons toasted sesame seeds

Place frozen meatballs in the refrigerator the night before to defrost. Put defrosted meatballs in Crock-Pot/slow cooker set at high heat. Cover with 1/2 to 2/3 bottle of Shanghai BBQ sauce and cook with the lid on for 15 to 25 minutes or when the sauce starts to bubble, turn the heat to low and you can let this simmer for hours, but the smell will drive you crazy! To serve, remove cover and sprinkle toasted sesame seeds over the top. Place a toothpick holder with plenty of toothpicks next to the Crock-Pot and everyone can spear their own hot meatballs—or you can serve them on platter, "real fancy like." Now that was a hard dish to make!

Options: crushed pineapple (drained)
Use Smokin' Willie's Classic or Fiesta BBQ Sauces

5 minutes to prep
1 to 4 hours in the Crock-Pot

This recipe is a wonderful appetizer that can be served at potlucks, Super Bowl Parties, over a bed of rice, or as hors d'oeuvres. This recipe could not be any easier to make. You can make your own meatballs with chicken, turkey, or beef; I do this for a small batch. I use frozen meatballs from a club store or supermarket in a slow cooker or Crock-Pot for larger groups. This is also a recipe I use for demos when I sample Smokin' Willie's Sauces. This recipe will give you plenty of time to get dolled up for the party!

Suggested Listening:

Hollywood Swinging
  Kool & The Gang
Take It To the Limit *The Eagles*
The Thrill Is Gone *B.B. King*
A Night In Tunisia *Charlie Parker*
Fun, Fun, Fun *The Beach Boys*
Hold Out Your Hand *Billy Squire*
Tainted Love/Where Did Our Love
  Go *Soft Cell*
Pipeline *The Chantays*
Brass In Pocket *The Pretenders*
The House Is Rockin'
  Stevie Ray Vaughn & Double Trouble

Shanghai Shrimp on a Stick

2 to 3 pounds of shrimp

(the larger the shrimp, the less time spent putting them on skewers); shelled & deveined is easier, but some prefer with the shell on. I use whichever is freshest or on sale.

1 lemon cut into wedges

Salt

Pepper

½ cup Smokin' Willie's Shanghai BBQ Sauce

8 to 12 skewers

depending on the size of the shrimp. If you use bamboo skewers soak in water for 30 minutes before assembly to keep from burning the ends.

Soak skewers. Wash shrimp and pat dry. Thread shrimp on skewers, tail to head with the main body of the shrimp alternating on each side of the skewer—one facing left and the next one facing right. Squeeze lemon juice lightly over the shrimp and season with salt and pepper.

This recipe is a quick cook. Expect to stay by the grill for at least 15 minutes. Get the grill going to medium high heat, and just before you start cooking, lightly wipe the grill with olive oil using a paper towel with long tongs. Place skewers on the grill (without any sauce on them yet) for 4 to 6 minutes, depending on the heat and the thickness of the shrimp. Turn over and brush on Smokin' Willie's Shanghai BBQ Sauce. When just cooked through, turn over indirect heat and brush with additional BBQ Sauce. Serve hot over a bed of brown or white rice with a salad and vegetables. If there are any leftovers, you can use them to make a quick and easy shrimp salad. Try using this Shanghai BBQ Sauce as a salad dressing.

Option: fish, beef, pork, chicken breasts (boneless & skinless) cut into strips to be threaded on skewers, a la Thai Sate. Try Classic or Fiesta BBQ Sauce for a different flavor.

15 minutes prep
15 minutes grilling time

Chef Michael Acuna created this dish when he was developing the Shanghai BBQ Sauce. We would use shrimp in this recipe most of the time, but you can also use chicken, beef, or pork. Quick and easy, and oh so tasty! This recipe is mobile so you can prepare it to be grilled at the park or bring it to a party at a friend's house. The sticks can be grilled or cooked on the stove; I even cook this recipe on an electric George Foreman Grill when I do food demos. These Shanghai sticks are always a crowd-pleaser!

Suggested Listening:

Turning Japanese *The Vapors*
Everybody Is a Star
  Sly And The Family Stone
Lunar Sea *Camel*
Message In a Bottle *The Police*
Fascination Street *The Cure*
Sweet Soul Music *Arthur Conley*
Imagine *John Lennon*
In the Mood
  Glenn Miller & His Orchestra
(Love Is Like A) Heat Wave
  Martha Reeves & The Vandellas
Day Dreaming *David Sanborn*

side dishes

BBQ Chicken Salad

1 pound cooked chicken or turkey

2 stalks celery diced

2 tablespoons Smokin' Willie's Classic BBQ Sauce

2 tablespoons mayonnaise

1 tablespoon Smokin' Willie's Classic Spice Rub

Salt

Pepper

Mix BBQ sauce, mayo, and spices in a bowl using a fork; use more or less BBQ sauce and mayonnaise to taste. Dice and/or pull apart cooked poultry and place in the bowl with sauce. Add diced celery and mix to coat well. Keep refrigerated until ready to use.

Additional Recommendations:
Pickle relish
Basil
Green onion
Red onion
Ranch dressing instead of mayonnaise, especially for use as salad dressing

Southwest BBQ Salad: Use Smokin' Willie's Fiesta BBQ Sauce and New Mexico Spice Rub in the recipe for a spicy kick!

Sourdough bread with lettuce and tomato grilled on the George Foreman offers a tasty sandwich.

10 minutes prep

This is a unique recipe that uses leftover chicken or turkey to make a flavorful BBQ Chicken Salad. This recipe is a great use for leftover roasted whole chickens that you get pre-cooked from the store. After a couple of days of leftover Thanksgiving turkey I often make this recipe for a welcome change of flavor. Now I have to make sure that I make this BBQ salad before I run out of turkey! I pull or shred the meat with my hands if I am going to make sandwiches, and I dice the meat with a knife for salads. Adjust the seasonings, mayo, and BBQ sauce to satisfy your taste buds and enjoy!

Suggested Listening:

Strange Brew *Cream*
Still Crazy After All These Years
   Paul Simon
Gates of Steel *Devo*
It Don't Mean a Thing (If It Ain't
   Got That Swing) *Duke Ellington*
Another Country *Shadowfax*
I Like To Move It *Reel To Reel*
Willie and the Hand Jive
   The Johnny Otis Show
Sad But True *Metallica*
Sweetness Follows *R.E.M.*
(Let Me Up) I've Had Enough
   Kenny Wayne Shepherd

Bicna's BBQ Pork Salad

2 pounds center cut pork chops or pork butt

¾ cup Smokin' Willie's Shanghai BBQ Sauce

2 tablespoons sesame oil

1 tablespoon fish sauce

2 green onions, finely chopped

2 garlic cloves, finely chopped

Big, red leaf lettuce, or your favorite lettuce

Cilantro

Vietnamese or Thai basil

Mint leaves

Sliced cucumber

Mix BBQ sauce, sesame oil, fish sauce, green onions, and garlic and then marinade pork chops overnight. Grill over medium high heat 5 to 7 minutes a side, depending on the thickness and the heat, until cooked. Let pork chops rest, then thinly slice. Serve over a bed of crisp lettuce and cucumbers and garnish with cilantro or mint leaves.

Place sliced meat onto a big whole red lettuce leaf, with fresh sprigs of cilantro, greens, and sliced cucumber. Wrap it all up and dip into dipping sauce.

Dipping Sauce

Mix together:
1 cup water
¼ cup fish sauce
¼ cup lime juice, fresh squeezed
¼ cup sugar
2 cloves garlic crushed
Crushed red chiles to taste

Serving Suggestions: Serve with steamed rice, stuffed shiitake mushrooms, Shanghai BBQ ribs, stir fry, or ahi tuna.

15 minutes prep
20 minutes on the grill

Here is another flavorful recipe from our great friend Bicna. The Vietnamese love to grill; in fact, most Asian cultures have been grilling over charcoal and wood for eons. I wanted to add this recipe to the book because of the amazing flavor and textures, and Bicna adapted her family recipe with Smokin' Willie's Shanghai BBQ Sauce. Fish sauce has a distinct flavor and is used in Vietnamese and Thai cooking. You can find fish sauce in the Asian section of most supermarkets, but you can substitute soy sauce if you cannot find any. When I took Thai cooking classes in 1984, I would have to go to a Thai market to get most of the ingredients like sriracha hot sauce, chile paste, and fish sauce, but today these ingredients can be found in most markets. Bicna suggests making great tasting spare ribs using this recipe. Using pork chops is much quicker and easier than a pork rump.

This recipe is like the Chicken Lettuce Wrap, but with thin sliced pork. This dish is easy and satisfying for a hot summer evening meal. Fresh herbs complement the flavor, and you can use the Shanghai BBQ sauce for dipping. Bicna's BBQ Pork Salad can be a little messy, but isn't that what BBQ's all about?

"The Vietnamese enjoy most salads more like a lettuce wrap. We wrap egg rolls in leaves of red lettuce along with fresh herbs like basil, mint, cilantro, and then dip them in the sauce as well. It may be a messy ordeal the first time you try this recipe, but it's truly worth it!"

Suggested Listening:

Rhapsody in Blue *Gershwin*
Green Earrings *Steely Dan*
Cockatoo *Spyro Gyra*
Swing *Django Reinhardt*
More Than This *Roxy Music*
Papa's Got a Brand New Bag *James Brown*
In-A-Gadda-Da-Vida *Iron Butterfly*
Fire & Rain *James Taylor*
Ain't Nobody's Business *Jimmy Witherspoon*
Shooting Star *Bad Company*

Michael's Potato Salad

6 or 7 boiled potatoes, peeled and diced

5 eggs hard-boiled, chopped

1 cup celery, chopped

½ cup onion, chopped

½ cup pickle relish

Salt

Pepper

Mayonnaise

¼ cup Smokin' Willie's Classic BBQ Sauce

Mix together all of the ingredients until well coated, adding BBQ sauce a little at a time to taste. Refrigerate overnight to let the flavors develop.

35 to 45 minutes to boil the potatoes
20 minutes to make

Chef Michael Acuna developed this recipe using his mother's amazing potato salad recipe and Smokin' Willie's Classic BBQ sauce. At first I thought that this recipe sounded crazy, but once I tasted it I was hooked. If you like spicy, use Smokin' Willie's Fiesta with Chipotle BBQ sauce instead of the Classic sauce.

You can use your favorite family potato salad recipe to make this dish, or spice up one from the store. I am using a potato salad recipe that I got from my good friend Dean LaValley. Dean tells me that this is his grandmother Evelyn's recipe, also known lovingly as Mam-Maw.

Suggested Listening:

Let's Go Crazy *Prince*
Still Crazy After All These Years
  Ray Charles
Clocks *Coldplay*
You Really Got Me *The Kinks*
We Will Rock You *Queen*
Mister Magic *Grover Washington Jr.*
Brick House *Commodores*
Take This Job and Shove It
  Johnny Paycheck
Django *The Modern Jazz Quartet*

Mom's BBQ Baked Beans

**1 large can of each of the following:
pinto,
kidney, and
pork & beans**

Onion: ½ cup dehydrated or 1 fresh, chopped
(Mom uses dehydrated)

1 cup or more Smokin' Willie's Classic BBQ Sauce

1 bushel of love

Mom makes her BBQ baked beans in a Dutch oven but tells me that you can use a casserole dish or oven-proof pot. Now here comes the hard part … empty contents of the three cans with their juices into the Dutch oven or another container. Add the onion. Pour in Smokin' Willie's Classic BBQ Sauce to taste, starting with ½ cup. Mom's taste runs towards more like half of the bottle. Stir with lots of "love & good intentions."

Place in oven at 250 to 275 degrees uncovered until thickened and the smell drives everyone in the house absolutely crazy. This will take 2 ½ to 4 hours, depending on how thick you like your "Mom's BBQ Baked Beans." Mom says the "thicker the better," and this takes about 3½ to 4 hours.

Tastes great hot or cold. Picnics, tailgates, potlucks, "family gets" (get-togethers)—this recipe travels well and the beans are just as good the next day if not better, so you can make them ahead of time.

Serve with Mom's "Crew Q" menu, Smokin' Willie's Chicken, Pulled Pork, Dad's Steak, and Camping.

10 minutes prep
Cooks in oven 3 to 4 hours

This is another golden gem from my mother's kitchen. It is a recipe that has been with the family for as long as my mom can remember. Mom taught me the invaluable lesson of cooking things "her way," which means taking a recipe, following it exactly just once, and then making it "your own" by adding more of the things you like and taking away some of the things you like less. Mom's BBQ Baked Beans are just as anticipated as Mom's "Crew Q." Mom told me that at every potluck or family gathering, people would ask her if she brought her famed BBQ baked beans, especially Uncle George. This is another easy recipe that tastes great and can be made for larger groups.

Suggested Listening:

Silky, Silky, Soul Sender *Marvin Gaye* (Mom's Pick)
Mama's Cooking *Marcia Ball*
Red Beans *Red Garland*
Be-Bop *Charlie Parker*
Sweet Soul Sister *The Cult*
Live Wire *AC/DC*
Memphis Soul Stew *King Curtis*
Give Me Just a Little More Time *Chairmen of the Board*
Piece of My Heart *Big Brother and the Holding Company*
Great Balls of Fire *Jerry Lee Lewis*

Southwestern Wild Rice Stuffing

2 packages wild rice with seasonings

1½ pounds turkey sausage

4 stalks celery

1 large onion

Broth made from giblets or store-bought broth (turkey, chicken, or vegetable)

2 tablespoons Smokin' Willie's New Mexico Spice Rub

1 cup pecan pieces

Follow the directions on the packages to make the wild rice, replacing the water with turkey broth, in a pot big enough to mix all of the ingredients.

Preheat oven to 350 degrees. Break apart sausage and brown in a skillet. Drain the liquid and add the cooked sausage to the wild rice.

Sauté onion and after a few minutes add celery; sauté until onions are clear, then add to the wild rice mixture.

Add Smokin' Willie's New Mexico Spice Rub and chopped pecans and mix well. Put wild rice in a greased casserole dish or foil trays. Cover with foil and bake for 1 hour.

25 minutes prep
1 hour in the oven

I learned about this recipe early one morning the day before Thanksgiving, 1988. I was feeding my youngest son, Nick, to let his mom get some much-needed sleep. He was six months old at the time and I was watching a food show while Nick was in my arms having his bottle. The cook was making a wild rice stuffing and it looked really good, but I could not write anything down during the show—try taking a bottle out of the mouth of a baby in the middle of a feeding! After Nick was finished, burped, changed, and was content, I wrote down what I could remember and made my version that Thanksgiving. Well, this recipe is so good I have been making it ever since. In fact, Tia Vera would always request that I make extra for her to take home (makes great leftovers). This easy recipe can be made all year long for potlucks and family functions.

I started off using Uncle Ben's Wild Rice. I make the broth with turkey giblets and neck, but if you are going to use them for another recipe you can use store-bought chicken or turkey broth. I prefer turkey. I use spicy breakfast turkey sausage—we like it spicy, but if you don't you can use any type of sausage that you prefer (sweet Italian, breakfast, or pork). To go with the holiday turkey, I use turkey sausage. I also add 3 tablespoons of Smokin' Willie's New Mexico Spice Rub (again, we like it spicy). Taste the dish and finish seasoning before putting it in the pan. I use foil trays because this makes it easier during clean-up. I do not stuff my turkey because the turkey will cook faster and more evenly than if you stuff the bird, but you can still use this recipe for stuffing your turkey if you prefer.

Suggested Listening:

Holiday *Madonna*
Take Me In Your Arms (Rock Me A Little While)
  Kim Weston
I'm Getting Sentimental Over You *Tommy Dorsey*
I Got My Mojo Working *Muddy Waters*
Save It for Later *The English Beat*
The Neighborhood *Los Lobos*
Walk This Way *Run D.M.C.*
If You Don't Know Me By Now
  Harold Melvin And The Blue Notes
Give Peace a Chance *John Lennon*
Waltz In D Flat *Chopin*

Twin's Corn Bread

1½ cups all-purpose flour (unbleached)

1 cup cornmeal

2 teaspoons baking powder

¼ teaspoon baking soda

¾ teaspoon salt

¾ cup corn

¼ cup brown sugar

2 eggs

1 cup buttermilk

1 stick butter unsalted, melted

Place the cast iron skillet in the middle rack of the oven and preheat to 400 degrees.

Mix together the flour, cornmeal, baking powder, baking soda, and salt in a mixing bowl.

In a blender or food processor, mix the corn, brown sugar, buttermilk, and eggs. While the blender is running add the melted butter. Pour blended liquid into the dry ingredients and mix together until just moistened; do not over-mix.

Butter the baking dish, or spray the dish with a non-stick spray. In some cases you may not need to coat a well-seasoned cast iron skillet because of the butter in the recipe; every time that I have made it the corn bread comes right out.

Bake until golden brown; test by inserting a toothpick in the middle—it should come out clean after 25 to 35 minutes. With an iron skillet, the longer you leave it in the oven the thicker the crust. Cool for 10 minutes, if you can wait that long. Slice and serve with honey butter. If you have kids or a hungry crew, you might want to make two batches, because you may not have any left for the meal once they smell this corn bread baking in the oven.

15 minutes prep
25 to 35 minutes baking time

I did not know that there were so many corn bread recipes; it seems everyone has one that is a little different than the next. There are different flavors and textures; light, sweet, dense, spicy, and with cheese. This recipe is a mixture of two that were my grandmother's and her twin sister Lupe's. Grandma's was lighter and a little sweeter, and Auntie Lupe's recipe was more from the South—denser and using fresh corn in the ingredients. Tia Vera made an amazing corn bread with fresh corn, grated cheddar cheese, and diced green Ortega chiles (you can use them from a can to save time). Tia Vera would bake her corn bread in an iron skillet in the oven and the aroma was out of this world. Her corn bread was flavorful and thick with a lot of texture from the corn and chiles.

I like to roast an ear of corn on the grill and use it in this recipe, but it's not necessary to grill the corn. Frozen corn can be used when you cannot find any fresh; make sure to let it thaw before using in the recipe. Lately I have been using blue cornmeal, but you can use yellow or white. I am including this recipe because after trying many different corn breads, I think this one goes best with BBQ, although my family also enjoys this recipe with soups and many other meals.

There is also an easy-to-make recipe for honey butter that tastes great with corn bread; if there is any left over you can use it on toast. I use a cast iron skillet that my grandmother gave me when I purchased my first home, but you can use a glass or metal baking dish when baking this dish. The iron skillet, however, gives the corn bread a thicker crust. I can tell you that there is nothing like the smell of this corn bread baking and eating it hot, fresh out of the oven with honey butter. I am told that you can cook corn bread on the BBQ in the iron skillet, but I have never tried it. I usually do not have enough room on the grill.

Mom's Quick Corn Bread

Double Batch for the Crew

2 boxes Jiffy Corn Muffin Mix

¼ cup granulated sugar

¼ cup all-purpose flour

"Follow instructions on the package. Be sure to double what it says on one package, but add the amount of sugar and flour in the recipe," so says Mom!

5 minutes to prep
25 to 35 minutes baking

This is my mom's recipe that she has been making for many years. I know because I have a recipe card that Mom made for me over 25 years ago. It does not get any easier than this; naturally, this recipe comes from a woman who had five ever-hungry sons.

Suggested Listening:

Jubilee *Spyro Gyra*
You Need Love *Muddy Waters*
Flight of the Bumble Bee
　Rimsky-Korsakov
Give the People What They Want
　The O'Jays
The One *Foo Fighters*
Talk To Ya Later *The Tubes*
Hello Darlin' *Conway Twitty*
Sit Yourself Down *Stephen Stills*
Have I Told You Lately *Rod Stewart*

¼ cup honey

1 stick butter

¼ teaspoon water

Honey Butter

Fill measuring cup with hot water for 1 minute. Pour out the water and immediately measure the honey and pour in a mixing bowl. Less honey tends to stick to the measuring cup this way. Add the room temperature butter and water to the honey and whip with an electric mixer for 1 to 2 minutes or until completely smooth. Serve at room temperature. Store any leftover honey butter in the refrigerator.

10 minutes to prep

GRILLED VEGGIES

Smokin' Willie's List of Grillin' Veggies:

Asparagus

Broccoli

Carrots

Cauliflower

Chiles

Corn on the cob

Eggplant

Mushrooms

Onions

Peppers

Potatoes

Squash

Sweet Potatoes

Tomatoes

Zucchini

And the list goes on …

Quick and easy or low and slow, there are many ways to grill vegetables. Firmer and thicker veggies will take longer to grill (potatoes, corn, carrots) than softer and smaller vegetables (mushrooms, asparagus, eggplant).

Marinating vegetables is a simple process and I also use the marinade to brush on the vegetables while I am grillin'.

10 to 15 minutes prep
Grilling time varies depending on the veggies

I love to grill vegetables! By themselves with a light coating of olive oil, to a mixture of marinated vegetables in a kabob. From asparagus to zucchini, we all can use more vegetables in our diets, and here is a flavorful way to add them. The choice of vegetables and fruits in our stores is amazing, and with global transportation we have longer seasons and more variety to choose from.

Suggested Listening:

Harvest Moon *Neil Young*
Love Rollercoaster *Ohio Players*
She Drives Me Crazy
 Fine Young Cannibals
Hang on Sloopy *The McCoys*
It's Summertime *George Duke*
Teach Your Children
 Cosby, Stills, Nash & Young
Going To the Country
 The Steve Miller Band
Your Red Wagon *Red Garland*
Just Squeeze Me *Duke Ellington*
Virtue *Alphonse Mouzon*

BBQ Potatoes

1 pound
new potatoes

2 to 3 tablespoons
olive oil

1 to 2 tablespoons
Smokin' Willie's
New Mexico
spice rub

Salt

Pepper

Grilled New Potatoes

Wash and quarter the potatoes and place in a bowl. Coat the potatoes with the olive oil, spice rub, salt, and pepper. Add 1 to 2 tablespoons of olive oil and toss the potatoes to lightly coat. Only add enough olive oil to coat; too much and the oil drips on the fire and causes flare-ups. Add the spice rub to taste. I personally like a good coating of spices. Put the potatoes on the grill over direct heat. Turn the potatoes with a spatula or tongs as they brown, about 3 to 5 minutes a side, depending on the heat, until browned on all sides. If the potatoes are browned the way you like them, but are not cooked all the way, just move them over to the indirect heat side of the grates until cooked through.

5 minutes prep
20 to 30 minutes on the grill

Baked French Fries

Easy side dish for hamburgers, sandwiches, and steaks. Use frozen French fries—I use crinkle cut—and place on a rimmed cookie sheet. Sprinkle Smokin' Willie's New Mexico Spice Rub over the frozen French fries and bake in the oven at 450 for about 10 to 20 minutes or longer, depending on how crispy you like your French fries cooked. These are lower in fat than fries that have been fried in oil.

My son Nick used BBQ sauce to dip his French fries. Put BBQ sauce in a microwavable bowl and heat covered for 25 to 35 seconds, just to heat up, and serve warm for dipping.

10 to 20 minutes

I have cooked this recipe in a cast iron skillet for years and one night while I cooking up a batch of these potatoes I thought it would work on the grill. I am always thinking "can I grill this?" It worked and tasted great! There are many different colors and varieties of these small potatoes to choose from.

Grilled Baked Potatoes and Yams

1 potato per person

Toppings:

Butter
(Grillin' Butter recipe page 94)

Cheese

Sour cream

Plain yogurt

Chives or green onions

Mushrooms

Bacon bits

Shrimp

Ham

Dream on …

Wash potatoes, score an X across the top of the spud with a knife, and wrap with foil. Place potatoes over high, direct heat and turn every 3 or 4 minutes with tongs. After 4 turns, move over indirect heat for about 45 minutes or until cooked through. Carefully remove from foil and serve right away while steaming hot.

For sweet potatoes or yams, mix brown sugar and butter for a sweet alternative; adding a marshmallow to melt on top enhances the flavor even more.

Brown Sugar Butter

½ cube butter (room temperature)
3 tablespoons brown sugar
½ teaspoon water

In a bowl mix ingredients with an electric mixer for about 2 minutes.

Great on toast! Add a large marshmallow sliced in half placed on top (optional).

5 minutes prep
45 to 55 minutes grill time
10 minutes for the Brown Sugar Butter

If you can bake a potato, sweet potato, or yam in the oven, you can cook it on the grill. They take almost an hour to cook so put them on the grill first. With all of the things you can top potatoes with, they can be a meal all by themselves. Potatoes, yams, and sweet potatoes all use the same method for cooking.

Suggested Listening:

Potato Head Blues *Louis Armstrong*
I Like It Like That *Jerry Lee Lewis*
Freedom of Choice *Devo*
Welcome to the Jungle
  Guns 'N' Roses
Tighten Up *Archie Bell & The Drells*
A Forest *The Cure*
I Second That Emotion
  Smokey Robinson & The Miracles
Pick Up the Pieces
  Average White Band
All the Time *Jack Green*
Dream On *Aerosmith*

side dishes

Grilled Asparagus

1 pound asparagus

Balsamic vinegar & olive oil marinade (page 97)

1 tablespoon sesame seeds (optional)

Wash and trim the tough bottom of the asparagus stalks. Peel lower part of stalks of any larger sized asparagus with a potato peeler; leave the peel on thinner asparagus. Place the prepared asparagus in a gallon Ziploc® bag or covered container with the marinade and sesame seeds—let sit overnight for more flavor. Grill over medium high heat and baste with marinade and turn every couple of minutes until cooked through, depending on the size of the asparagus and the heat. Place asparagus thickest part over the hottest heat, with the tips over indirect heat. Do not overcook. Pick up one with tongs by the thick end and the tip should bend a little, not all the way. Use any leftover marinade as a tasty low-calorie salad dressing.

For the microwave, follow the directions for preparing the asparagus and place in microwavable dish. Cover with Saran™ wrap, poke a few holes in the Saran™ wrap to let steam escape. Microwave for 3 to 5 minutes depending on how powerful your microwave is. Let stand for 1 minute and then carefully remove Saran™ wrap. Serve immediately while hot.

10 minute prep
5 to 10 minutes on the grill

What a great vegetable to grill, and this is one of the vegetable recipes I get the most requests for! Starting with the spring in time for Mother's Day on through the summer, I grill seasonal asparagus quite a bit. This recipe can be done in the microwave in about 4 minutes if in a pinch, or in a skillet on the stove.

Suggested Listening:

Hot House *Charlie Parker*
Mother Earth *Memphis Slim*
Just Can't Get Enough *Depeche Mode*
Tell Me Something Good *Rufus*
Dancing Days *Led Zeppelin*
Here Comes the Sun *The Beatles*
To Turn You On *Roxy Music*
Peace on Earth … Mother Earth … 3rd Stone from the Sun *Santana*
Once You've Had the Best *George Jones*
Graceland *Paul Simon*

side dishes

Grilled Corn on the Cob

2 ears fresh corn

Southwestern Grillin' Butter
(recipe page 94)

Salt

Pepper

Smokin' Willie's New Mexico Spice Rub

Foil

Southwestern Grillin' Corn

Remove husks and silk from ears of corn and wash. Melt Grillin' Butter in microwave. Either break an ear of corn with your hands, or score around the center of the corn to make it easier to break in half, or leave them whole. Put the two pieces together where they broke apart and place on a piece of foil. Brush with melted Grillin' Butter and sprinkle New Mexico Spice Rub, salt, and pepper on the corn. Wrap the ear of corn in the foil, making sure to seal the ends. If you are doing this ahead of time, place in refrigerator.

When you are ready to cook the corn, place it over high heat and turn every 2 minutes, 4 or 5 times. Move over indirect heat and then turn corn every time you lift the lid. Brush a little more butter and sprinkle Smokin' Willie's New Mexico Spice Rub, if needed, on the corn as you serve your meal.

Use any extra corn on salads. Just stand the corn on end and slice the kernels from the cob with a sharp knife.

10 minutes to prep
25 to 30 minutes of grill time.

Corn has to be the all time grillin' staple of vegetables. I have two recipes for corn on the cob for you to try: one on the grill and one for larger groups (like Mom's Crew Q) done on the stove top. On the grill I usually wrap the corn in foil. You can also remove all of the husk and silk and then lightly coat your corn with olive oil or butter and sprinkle on salt, pepper, and seasonings and place right on the grill. I use the foil wrapped recipe quite a bit so that I can prep it the night before, then take it out of the fridge about a half hour before I put it on the grill.

You can break the ears of corn in half to make it easier to eat; plus, not everyone will want a whole ear. I prefer white corn when it's seasonal, but there are tasty bi-colored varieties. It's good to get your corn fresh, directly from the farmer's market! Here is another recipe that you can prepare ahead of time and is great for camping and tailgating.

side dishes

Smokin' Corn for a Crew

Corn on the cob

Butter

Smokin' Willie's New Mexico Spice Rub

Salt

Pepper

Remove husk and silk from ears of corn. Break or cut the ears in half, or leave whole and place in a large pot. Cover corn with water and add 1 tablespoon of salt. Cover and bring to a boil. Let boil for 10 minutes, then turn off the heat and let the pot stand for about 10 minutes. With pot holders carefully drain the water from the pot and while corn is still steaming hot, add butter and seasoning. With the cover on and using pot holders, shake the pot to coat corn with butter and seasonings. Serve right away and enjoy the summer flavor of corn on the cob with your meal!

20 minutes prep
15 to 20 minutes on the stove

This is a great recipe for a larger group of people. I have done fifteen ears of corn at one time for a family gathering of about twenty-five people. You can clean the ears ahead of time and store in the fridge.

Suggested Listening:

Beautiful Day *U2*
It's Summer *The Temptations*
Sweet Emotion *Aerosmith*
Someone, Somewhere In the Summertime *Simple Minds*
Everything Is Coming Our Way *Santana*
Wherever I May Roam *Metallica*
Goodbye Yellow Brick Road *Elton John*
Suavecito *Malo*
Shake It Baby *John Lee Hooker*
Butterfly *Crazytown*
Sweet Jane *Lou Reed*

Grilled Garlic

1 head garlic

Salt

Pepper

1/2 teaspoon olive oil

—

Garlic Bread Spread

Grilled garlic

Salt

Pepper

1 cube sweet butter (room temperature)

1 teaspoon dried basil

1 teaspoon dried parsley

1 teaspoon Smokin' Willie's New Mexico Spice Rub (optional)

¼ teaspoon Worcestershire sauce

¼ teaspoon water

¼ cup parmesan and/or Romano cheese (optional)

Carefully slice the top ¼ of the head of garlic, leaving the skin on, and place in the center of a square of foil. Lifting the top of the garlic that you just cut, drizzle olive oil on top and sprinkle with salt and pepper. Wrap garlic head tightly with foil. Bake at 375 degrees in the oven for 30 to 45 minutes, or grill over indirect heat for 30 to 45 minutes. Let the garlic cool for 10 to 15 minutes in the foil wrap. Remove from the foil and squeeze out the cooked garlic into a bowl to be used in different recipes, or simply spread on a fresh baguette.

5 minutes prep
40 minutes to grill or bake

—

Garlic Bread Spread

Place all ingredients in food processor or in a mixing bowl and whip with an electric beater until well mixed. Use at room temperature for easy spreading. You can store the flavored butter in a dish or Tupperware® and store in the refrigerator for later use.

Great on vegetables!

1 order of the garlic recipe and 5 minutes to process

Grilling a head of garlic on the BBQ is like roasting it in the oven. Cooking garlic smoothes out the flavor and makes a great addition to dips and spreads. Used in the basil mayonnaise, garlic bread spread, and vegetable spread/dip or by itself on a fresh baguette with soft cheese will make your mouth water. The smell of cooking garlic on the grill is out of this world and will make heads turn when they catch a whiff.

Suggested Listening:

I Got You (I Feel Good) *James Brown*
In the Air Tonight *Phil Collins*
Love Shack *The B-52's*
Johnny B. Goode *Chuck Berry*
I Ain't Superstitious *Jeff Beck*
Larks' Tongues In Aspic
 King Crimson
Shine On You Crazy Diamond
 Pink Floyd
That'll Be the Day *Linda Ronstadt*
Afterglow *Genesis*
Slow Slide *Fourplay*

GRILLED MUSHROOMS AND PORTOBELLO & FRESH CHEESE SANDWICHES

4 large Portobello mushrooms,
1 per person

Balsamic Vinegar and Olive Oil Marinade
(see page 97)

Fresh hamburger buns or hoagie rolls

Fresh mozzarella cheese

Sliced tomatoes

Sliced red onion (grilled)

Lettuce

Grilled Vegetable Spread
(see page 96)

**and/or
Basil Garlic Mayonnaise**
(see page 92)

This is our version of the veggie burger. My son Matt told me that this sandwich is better than a hamburger any day.

Portobello and Fresh Cheese Sandwiches
Wash mushrooms with a brush and trim the stem flush with the cap, so that bottom of mushroom lays flat on the grill. Place mushrooms and marinade in a gallon Ziploc® bag or in Tupperware® to marinate for 1 to 4 hours; if you leave them in the marinade too long they will get soggy. Slice tomatoes and onions, clean the lettuce, and then slice fresh mozzarella. Grill over medium high heat; be careful, since the oil in the marinade can flare up. Cook for 10 to 15 minutes, depending on the size of the mushrooms and the heat of the grill, turning once halfway through. Grill onions at the same time as the mushrooms for these sandwiches because they take the same amount of time to cook. Slice extra mushrooms for rolls and leave whole for hamburger buns. Make the sandwiches your way and enjoy! Note: you will need extra napkins. Like a great hamburger, these sandwiches are juicy and can be a bit messy.

15 minutes prep
1 to 4 hours to marinade
10 to 20 minutes grill time

Next to corn, I grill mushrooms the most. Portobello mushroom sandwiches, kabobs, button mushrooms loose on the grill—the BBQ adds a great smoky flavor. The marinade I use for mushrooms, especially Portobellos, is the Balsamic Vinegar & Olive Oil (recipe on page 97). I find that the easiest way to clean mushrooms is with a vegetable brush. I clean and then trim the end of the stem, usually level with the cap so that it is easier to grill both sides. When I make shish kabobs I always marinate extra mushrooms for use in salads. When I grill vegetables, I almost always add mushrooms to the mix. I find that the firmer mushrooms (button, crimini, and shiitake) can be marinated overnight and the softer ones (Portobello, morels, and oyster) do not need as much time; an hour or more. Grill until the mushrooms soften, but don't go flat; 5 to 10 minutes on each side.

Suggested Listening:

Psychedelic Shack *The Temptations*
I Don't Need No Doctor *Humble Pie*
Running On Faith *Eric Clapton*
Dreamer *Tommy Bolin*
White Rabbit *Jefferson Airplane*
Dr. Feelgood
  Count Basie & His Orchestra
Moonage Daydream *David Bowie*
Wasted Days and Wasted Nights
  Freddy Fender
Double Vision *Foreigner*
Yin *Larry Coryell*

Grilled Onions

Onions

Brown Onions

Green Onions

Pearl Onions

Sliced for hamburgers or sandwiches, about ¼ inch thick, you can use red or brown onions. Grill about 3 minutes a side over direct heat; grilled tastes way better!

By themselves, slice off the ends, peel, and then quarter each onion. Place the quartered pieces cut side down. The onion will separate as it cooks on the grill. Turn to cook both sides, about 8 to 10 minutes.

Grilled pearl onions and cherry tomatoes are great for salads or on a bed of rice.

5 to 10 minutes prep

Grilled onions are great not just for hamburgers, but can be used to accompany other dishes. On kabobs with other mixed vegetables or by themselves, onions are simple to prepare and cook quickly. Red, brown, green, and pearl, there are many types of onions to cook on your grill.

Suggested Listening:

Green Onions *Booker T & The MG's*
Blue Suede Shoes *Elvis Presley*
Hold On Loosely *38 Special*
Can You Dig It *Grover Washington Jr.*
Zoot Allures *Frank Zappa*
Canary In a Coal Mine *The Police*
Fuel *Metallica*
Strange *The Living End*

Grilled Peppers

Bell Peppers

Chile Peppers

Bell Peppers

Wash and pierce the bottom and top with a knife (to release steam) and place on the grill whole. Grill for about 3 to 4 minutes a side; skin will bubble and char. Place in a paper bag for 10 to 15 minutes, as this makes it easier to peel off the skin. Remove from bag and peel off charred skin; remove seeds and stem and then slice into strips (amazing on a roast beef sandwich). Use on salads and sandwiches.

Bell Peppers Recipe #2

Wash and then slice, core, and seed bell pepper into strips or squares. Grill both sides over medium heat until soft but not mushy, about 2 to 3 minutes a side. Simple and tasty, this recipe is easy and delicious.

Chile Peppers

With care (you should use gloves when handling chiles), wash and pierce the ends of the chiles with a toothpick or a knife to release steam while cooking. (Note that I know someone who was grilling a batch of chiles and did not pierce them. A couple of chiles exploded and he was slightly burned, not from the heat of the fire but from the chiles.) Grill chiles until skin is charred and place them in a paper bag for 10 to 15 minutes to separate the skin and to cool off enough to handle. Again, with gloves, remove the charred skin and then core and seed the chiles. You can also use the charred chiles with the skin on to add a smoky flavor. Makes for a great salsa!

5 to 15 minutes prep
10 to 20 minutes to grill

Chiles and green, red, and yellow bell peppers have a depth of flavor that comes out from cooking on the grill. Chiles can be roasted for salsa, along with the onions and tomatoes. Bell peppers grilled with onions makes for a great sausage sandwich. Bell peppers are great with kabobs, mixed veggies, salads, and used to make a veggie spread.

Suggested Listening:

One Hot Minute
 The Red Hot Chili Peppers
The Glow *Bonnie Ratt*
Don't Stand So Close To Me
 The Police
Who Do You Love
 Ronnie Hawkin & The Hawks
(Love Is Like A) Heat Wave
 Martha & The Vandellas
Skin It Back *Little Feat*
Get Happy *Bud Powell Trio*

Mixed Veggies

2 yellow summer squash

2 zucchini

12 button mushrooms

1 medium red onion

12 cherry tomatoes

Balsamic Vinegar Recipe (page 97) or Italian salad dressing

1 tablespoon fresh basil, chopped

Salt

Pepper

Wash all of the veggies. Slice ends off of squash and zucchini, and slice lengthways into ¼-inch thick slices. Trim ends of onion, remove skin and quarter. Wash mushrooms with a brush and trim stems even with the bottom of the cap. Place all of the vegetables in a gallon Ziploc® baggie or covered Tupperware® and add vinegar/oil mixture or Italian salad dressing to cover. Marinate for 2 hours or longer. For fullest flavor, consider doing this the night before. Place onions, squash, and zucchini directly on the grill over medium heat with mushrooms and cherry tomatoes around the side. Turn after 5 to 10 minutes, depending on the heat and thickness of the veggies.

Serve on the side with BBQ chicken, Tri-Tip, or almost any dish—here is a tasty way to add veggies to your diet!

20 to 30 minutes prep
10 to 20 minutes of grillin'

This is a basic recipe that I use all of the time during the summer, especially with all of the fresh vegetables that are in season. I try to use ingredients that are the same texture or that will cook for the same amount of time. Cauliflower and eggplant will take different amounts of time to cook. Use leftover veggies in salads, or use them to make a roasted vegetable dip (page 96).

Suggested Listening:

You By My Side *Chris Squire*
I Believe *Bill Miller*
Rustle of Spring *Sinding*
I Will Follow *U2*
Turn In Time *Yellowjackets*
Back In the High Life Again
 Steve Winwood
Doctor, Doctor *UFO*
Always on My Mind *Willie Nelson*
People Get Ready *The Impressions*
I Can Hear Music *The Beach Boys*

sandwiches

Pulled Pork

1 boneless pork cushion roast, 4 to 5 pounds

Water to cover

2 onions quartered

1 garlic head

3 tablespoons Smokin' Willie's Spice Rub

2 tablespoons salt

1 tablespoon pepper

1 bottle Smokin' Willie's Classic BBQ Sauce

Fresh rolls or hamburger buns

Your favorite coleslaw

Rinse and clean meat with water and place in a large enough pot to cover with water about 3 to 4 inches above the top of the meat. Quarter onion and remove skin from the garlic and add to the pot, along with the spice rub, salt, and pepper. Bring to a boil, then let simmer for 2 to 3 hours depending on the size of the roast. The longer you cook it, the easier it is to pull the meat apart; waiting isn't easy because the smell is so good!

Remove from the pot when the roast starts to fall apart and let cool on a platter or place back in the pot after removing the liquid until the meat has cooled enough for you to "pull" the meat apart into smaller pieces by hand, making sure to remove any fat and gristle. Place "pulled" meat in a slow cooker or pan and sprinkle with Smokin' Willie's Spice Rub and cover with Smokin' Willie's Classic BBQ Sauce to taste. You now have one of the best BBQ sandwiches you have ever made!

Options:

Chicken: Use boneless breasts and thighs and boil until the meat is easily pulled apart. It will takes less time to cook than the pork.

Beef: I use whatever roast is on sale and cook it following this recipe.

Spicy: Use Smokin' Willie's New Mexico Spice Rub and Fiesta with Chipotle BBQ Sauce for a spicy kick.

Save a little of the meat and add Smokin' Willie's Shanghai BBQ Sauce and serve over rice or noodles for a unique Asian dish.

20 minute prep
2 to 3 hours simmering on the stove
30 minutes pulling pork

Suggested Listening:

Can't Get Enough *Bad Company*
Gimme Shelter *Grand Funk Railroad*
St. Louis Blues
   Louis Armstong & His Orchestra
Didn't I (Blow Your Mind This Time)
   The Delfonics
People Get Ready *Bob Marley*
Please, Please, Please *James Brown*
Something Inside Me *Elmore James*
Try a Little Tenderness *Otis Redding*
The Great Pretender *The Platters*
Polk Salad Annie *Tony Joe White*
Beer Drinkers and Hell Raisers *ZZ Top*
Brittany & Bailey's soccer team's pick:
We Are The Champions *Queen*

This is a different recipe than most for pulled pork because I do not smoke or BBQ the meat—it is boiled on top of the stove. The secret is in the Smokin' Willie's spices and the sauce. This is one of the more difficult and time-consuming recipes in this book, but it is guaranteed to be a hit every time and well worth all of the effort.

The recipe has evolved over the years and I was finally happy with it when I was asked to cook BBQ pork sandwiches for an AYSO soccer tournament that Bicna & Frank Bagheri do annually. The Bagheris also put on the best youth sporting event that I have ever witnessed, and they wanted something special to serve 300 volunteers and referees. The Bagheri's twin daughters, Brittany & Bailey, claimed that their soccer team won 1st Place in the championship game because they ate the pork sandwiches for lunch. They're also huge fans of Smokin' Willie's BBQ Sauce. I was told that some of the volunteers were fighting over the leftovers because it was so good! The refs and volunteers are still talking about how good the sandwiches were, six months after the soccer tournament! We've heard that some referees chanted, "We'll ref for Pulled Pork Sandwiches!"

I cooked the pulled chicken with Classic Sauce for The Mark & Brian Radio Show in Los Angeles, and Brian loved this recipe so much he asked me to save the rest for him and him only! Mark liked the spicy, fiesta with chipotle BBQ sauce. With this recipe you can cook for larger groups and parties, and it is great for Super Bowl gatherings. When it is too cold or too hot outside, you can still have BBQ, and you can also make this ahead of time and keep it warm in a slow cooker. Top with some coleslaw on a fresh roll or a hamburger bun, and wow, you are now in BBQ heaven! A hot dog bun works great for little kids. You can substitute pork with chicken or beef in this recipe.

Note: you will lose almost half the weight of the meat you are cooking. A six-pound roast will end up with just over three pounds of pulled meat. You can figure four to six sandwiches per cooked pound of meat depending on the size of your sandwiches. WARNING: You will want to make more than you think; these sandwiches are amazingly delicious and will go quickly.

BBQ Meatball Sandwich

3 pounds frozen meatballs (defrosted)

1 bottle Smokin' Willie's Classic BBQ Sauce

¾ pound sliced sandwich cheese (mozzarella)

10 hoagie buns

Place frozen meatballs in the refrigerator the night before to defrost. Put defrosted meatballs in a Crock-Pot/slow cooker set to high heat and pour in 1/2 to 2/3 bottle Smokin' Willie's Classic BBQ Sauce, enough to completely coat all of the meatballs. Reduce heat to low and simmer after 45 minutes to 1 hour, or when the sauce starts to bubble. You can actually let them simmer for hours, but that is just plain mean because the smell of this cooking indoors will drive everyone crazy! Place sliced cheese on the bun then spoon on the meatballs with the BBQ sauce.

5 minutes prep
1 to 3 hours in the Crock-Pot

Super Bowl Sunday, I was with Matt, Nick, and a bunch of their friends hosting a party, watching the big game, eating junk food, and drinking sodas. We sent Mom out shopping with the girls. Halftime rolls around and it was time for the BBQ Meatball Sandwiches out on the patio—these can be messy, so no way was I going to let a bunch of young men eat these sandwiches in the house. I had wet washcloths at hand to make sure these guys were wiped clean before returning inside to watch the rest of the game!

This recipe can be made ahead of time and brought to the next party or big game—football, hockey, soccer, baseball, or even badminton. These can also be used as appetizers with toothpicks. I use frozen meatballs or you can make them yourself using your own special recipe. Make sure you have plenty of napkins or paper towels on hand because these sandwiches are the kind that define the expression, "If it ain't messy, it ain't good."

Suggested Listening:

Super Bowl Sundae *Ozomatli*
Situation *Yaz*
Eminence Front *The Who*
Thunder & Lightning *Thin Lizzy*
Television Man *Talking Heads*
Stand By Me *Ben E. King*
You Wear It Well *Rod Stewart*
Son of Your Father *Elton John*
Bottle Up and Go *John Lee Hooker*
Trouble Every Day *Frank Zappa*

Mary & Mason's Grilled Cheese Sandwich

Sliced American cheese
(1 or 2 slices per sandwich)

Hamburger buns

Open the hamburger buns and toast the insides on the grill. Place 1 or 2 slices of cheese on the bottoms and then put the tops on. Grill bottoms down for 2 to 3 minutes, or until browned. Flip over with a spatula, press down lightly for another 2 to 3 minutes, or until browned on the second side. Let cool. The cheese will be hot right off the grill!

Try sprinkling a little Smokin' Willie's Spice Rub on the cheese as you make these sandwiches for a flavorful twist!

2 minutes prep
5 minutes on the grill

One summer afternoon we were having a simple, last-minute Family "Q" with hamburgers and hot dogs. Our nieces, Mary and Mason, asked for cheeseburgers without the meat. Alicia, their mom, said that they like cheese on a hamburger bun grilled on the BBQ. Well, after trying one, I found it to be tasty, and even a picky eater will like this sandwich! You can use different cheeses (Swiss, provolone, and mozzarella) and different breads (wheat or rye; sourdough is my favorite) for the adults—kids like them also!

Suggested Listening:

Hot Fun In the Summertime
  Sly And The Family Stone
Crazy Love *Van Morrison*
Ready for Love *Bad Company*
Stay Up Late *Talking Heads*
Why Not Me *The Judds*
Oh Girl *Chi-Lights*
Tip Toe Through the Tulips with Me
  Tiny Tim

Southwestern Spicy Chicken Burger

1 pound ground chicken

1 egg beaten

¼ cup crushed tortilla, nacho flavored chips or Fritos

1 tablespoon Smokin' Willie's New Mexico Spice Rub

¼ cup Smokin' Willie's Fiesta BBQ Sauce

4 hamburger buns or kaiser rolls

Options:

Cheese

Lettuce

Tomatoes

Grilled onions

Grilled Pasilla chiles

Grilled Salsa
(recipe page 15)

Crush chips with a rolling pin and set aside. Beat egg, BBQ sauce, and spice rub together. Mix together ground meat, chips, and egg mixture by hand until well incorporated. Makes 4 patties. Make sure to refrigerate until ready to grill. Grill over medium high heat until completely cooked through, about 5 to 7 minutes a side.

Serve with Grilled Salsa (page 15) and chips, baked French fries (page 36) or potato salad spiked with 2 tablespoons of Fiesta BBQ Sauce.

15 minutes prep
10 to 15 minutes on the grill

This is a spicy sandwich that I first tried with ground beef, though you can use turkey or bison as alternatives in this recipe. This recipe works really well for chicken and turkey because the egg and BBQ sauce hold this meat together. The bold flavors of the sauce and rub with the crumbled chips stand out compared with the bland flavor of chicken or turkey. This is basically chicken meatloaf patties with the onions and peppers on the outside. If you make the chicken patties ahead of time, make sure you refrigerate them right away.

Suggested Listening:

Chicken Strut *The Meters*
X & Y *Coldplay*
Golden Feather *Robbie Robinson*
Dreams *Fleetwood Mac*
Changes *Yes*
Reelin' In the Years *Steely Dan*
That's Life *Frank Sinatra*
Epistrophy *Thelonious Monk*
Whatcha See Is What You Get
   The Dramatics
Chicken Hearted Baby
   Clarence Samuels

Shanghai Turkey Burger

1 pound ground turkey

1 egg

¼ cup Smokin' Willie's Shanghai BBQ Sauce

¼ cup Panko crumbs or bread crumbs

1 green onion, diced

Salt

Pepper

4 sesame seed hamburger buns or kaiser rolls

Serving Suggestions:

Lettuce

Tomato

Onion

Smokin' Willie's Shanghai BBQ Sauce (On the bun)

In a mixing bowl, add egg and Shanghai BBQ Sauce and then whip together with a fork. Add ground turkey, Panko crumbs, green onion, salt, and pepper and mix all ingredients by hand until well incorporated. Divide the meat in to 4 equal balls. Form the patties with your hands; try not to over handle because this can toughen the burger. Grill over medium high heat for about 5 to 7 minutes per side or until completely cooked through. Serve hot right off the grill.

15 minutes preparation time
10 to 15 minutes on the grill

This tasty recipe is a great alternative for the regular hamburger. The Shanghai BBQ sauce helps bump up the flavor of the otherwise bland taste of ground turkey. Panko crumbs can be found in the Asian section of your local supermarket. The egg and Shanghai BBQ Sauce help hold together the ground turkey patties. When grilling you will want to use a medium to medium high heat and keep an eye on them; you will want to make sure to cook the turkey thoroughly without burning the outside.

Suggested Listening:

One of These Nights *The Eagles*
Free Range *Fourplay*
The Meaning Of Love *Depeche Mode*
Happy the Man *Genesis*
Sweet Child O' Mine *Guns N' Roses*
China Grove *The Doobie Brothers*
All Along the Watchtower
   Jimi Hendrix
Walking the Blues *Willie Dixon*
I Got It Bad and That Ain't Good
   Duke Ellington
Reach Out I'll Be There *The Four Tops*

Teriyaki Sandwich

2 to 2 ½ pounds top sirloin

¾ cup liquid aminos or soy sauce

¼ cup Mirin (sweet Japanese rice wine)

2 tablespoons sesame seeds

¼ cup brown sugar

Green onions, diced

Fresh French roll, hoagie roll, or soft sandwich roll

In a small saucepan heat to a simmer soy sauce, Mirin, and brown sugar, stirring until sugar is dissolved. Cool to room temperature while you prepare the rest of the ingredients.

Trim fat from around the edge of the top sirloin steak and then slice (against the grain) into ¼ inch thick strips. Place in a gallon Ziploc® baggie with sesame seeds and diced green onions. Pour in the cooled teriyaki sauce, remove as much air as possible, and seal. Place in the refrigerator overnight. You can freeze this recipe to take camping.

Grill over medium high heat until medium-rare, approximately 7 to 15 minutes. Serve on a soft hoagie roll and enjoy!

20 minutes prep
10 to 15 minutes grillin' time

This is one of my oldest recipes from the days when Diana and I would go to the Renaissance Fair back in the '70s. There was a sandwich that they served at the fair that was out of this world, and the recipe was not from the time of the Renaissance. You are outdoors walking around, and then you smell the delicious aroma of teriyaki permeating the air—it just drove me crazy. One of my best friends, Calvin Kawada's mother helped me with a couple of ingredients and I think this recipe is spot-on. Diana and I used to drive to the beach and cook this dish on a Hibachi; a lot of people would come by and ask what we were cooking because of the amazing smell. Great for a camping trip, on the stove, but best grilled. I use a top sirloin steak about 1 ½ to 2 inches thick, but you can use a London broil or flank steak for this recipe. When cutting the meat be sure to cut against the grain of the meat. This recipe works just as well with boneless/skinless chicken breast. I try to find the freshest, softest rolls to make this sandwich. This recipe feeds 6.

Suggested Listening:

Unbound *Robbie Robertson*
Sunshine of Your Love *Cream*
A Midsummer's Night's Dream:
  Spring Song *Mendelssohn*
Earth Angel *The Penguins*
And You and I *Yes*
The Best Is Yet To Come
  Grover Washington Jr.
Aja *Steely Dan*
Tell Her She's Lovely *El Chicano*
Los Angeles *X*
Jealous Again *The Black Crowes*

main dishes

T-Bone & Porterhouse Steak

1 T-Bone or porterhouse steak per person

1 tablespoon extra virgin olive oil or more if necessary to lightly coat the steak

1 tablespoon Smokin' Willie's Spice Rub

Lightly coat both sides of each steak with olive oil; I do this on a rimmed cookie sheet. Coat both sides of steak with Smokin' Willie's Spice Rub; my family likes a lot of rub on their steaks as it makes for an amazing crust and seals in the juices. Grill directly over a high-to-medium-high heat for 7 to 10 minutes and then flip, trying not to knock off too much of the spice rub. Do not press down on the meat while on the grill or use a fork and pierce the meat; you will lose precious juices. Instead use tongs or a spatula. Grill the other side for 5 to 7 minutes or more depending on the heat of the BBQ and how well done you desire your steak. Let the meat rest for 5 to 7 minutes under a foil tent before serving.

It seems like tradition that we serve baked potatoes, and a fresh green salad when we grill steaks. I like to grill asparagus (page 38) or corn on the cob (page 39) as the vegetable for the meal, but you can use whatever is in season. My sons use Smokin' Willie's Classic BBQ Sauce as a dipping sauce for their steak. I heat the sauce in a ramekin or small bowl in the microwave covered with a paper towel for 25 to 35 seconds, remove, and stir with a spoon. You can heat more if necessary.

5 minutes prep
15 to 25 minutes grillin' time

Here is where I would celebrate on payday or on a special occasion—by grilling porterhouse steaks from Luchesse's Italian market in the late 1970s. I like the porterhouse steak the best because it is the "King of steaks" and I like to grill meat that has the bone in. You get the filet meat in this cut that you do not get with the T-Bone steak. 1½ to 2 inches thick, grilled medium rare with a baked potato, salad, and garlic bread—this is a man's meal. This is also about the time I started developing the Smokin' Willie's award-winning Spice Rub, grilling steaks, and Tri-Tips. A coworker at Warner Bros. Records, Vince DiPierro, suggested that I lightly rub olive oil on the meat before seasoning it, and I have ever since. If someone that you are cooking for likes their meat well done, get them thinner steaks or ones that do not have the bone in them so that they will cook faster. Women can grill this for their men on Father's Day with ease. More women are grilling nowadays, which is why I recommend this recipe for a Father's Day menu that will impress any dad.

Suggested Listening:

T-Bone Blues *T-Bone Walker*
Just Got Paid Today *ZZ Top*
T-Bone Shuffle *Collins, Cray & Copeland*
Big Rub *Kevin Mahogany*
Hot Barbeque *Brother Jack McDuff*
Takin' Care of Business
  Bachman Turner Overdrive
Thank You *Led Zeppelin*
Hope Your Feeling Better *Santana*
Smoke Stack Lightnin' *Howlin' Wolf*
Just What I Needed *The Cars*
Jump In To the Fire *Metallica*
Express Yourself *Charles Wright & The
  Watts 103rd Street Rhythm Band*

Smokin' Willie's Ribs

2 racks baby back ribs

BBQ soak (recipe page 91)

2 tbsp. Smokin' Willie's Spice Rub

Smokin' Willie's Classic BBQ Sauce

Rinse off ribs, pat dry, and put on a cutting board meat side down, curve facing up. With the narrow end facing away from you take a knife and cut under the white membrane, just enough to grab. Using a paper towel, grip the membrane in one hand, and hold ribs with the other hand and peel the membrane off pulling towards you. Cut a rack of baby back ribs in half or three sections—it's easier to flip on the grill and cooks faster. Beef ribs I cut individually. Marinate with the BBQ soak, enough to cover ribs, then put overnight in the refrigerator.

Soak wood chips in water at least ½ hour before you put the ribs on the grill, if you are using them. Remove ribs from the soak and sprinkle meat side with the spice rub to taste; you can put spices on the membrane side but it seems to mostly fall off when you are cooking them on the grill. Just before putting ribs on the grill add the soaked wood chips. Sear the ribs directly over medium high heat. Start with the curved side down for about 8 to 10 minutes with the lid down and then turn over and grill until you have good color on the meat side. (Watch for flare-ups during this time.) Move ribs over indirect heat, curved side down, close the lid and cook for about 20 to 25 minutes. Do not open the lid because you will lose heat, and being over indirect heat you will not have any flare-ups. Turn ribs over and cook for another 15 to 20 minutes and close the lid. Brush Classic BBQ Sauce on both sides of the ribs over indirect heat and close the lid for 5 to 8 minutes. You do not want to overcook the ribs on the grill because you will finish cooking them in the oven.

Take the ribs right off the grill and put them in a roasting pan or foil tray, add more Classic BBQ Sauce to your taste. Seal the pan with foil and bake in the oven. Adjust the temperature to match how long until you are ready to serve:

325 for 30 to 45 minutes
300 for 45 to 60 minutes
275 for 1 to 1½ hours

This is one of the hardest recipes in this book and may seem like a lot of work but it is worth the effort and you will have grilled the most tender and great tasting ribs. If I ask someone what they want me to grill for them, they will almost always ask for my "baby back, baby back, baby back ribs."

30 minutes to prep
50 minutes to 1 hour on the grill
Finish off in the oven

This recipe is one of Mom's oldest and most requested. The secret is in Mom's soak recipe and removing the membrane from the backside of the ribs. In a pinch you do not have to soak the ribs, but the extra effort is well worth the added flavor and moisture. Mom would finish them in the oven in an old enameled roasting pan, and when she would pull them out of the oven and pull back the foil, she never had to call everyone for dinner—the smell of the BBQ ribs would drive everyone to the table.

There are so many ways to cook ribs that what people are always asking me when I have done demos is, "What is the best way to cook ribs?" Here is the Smokin' Willie's method—actually Mom's. This is the recipe for the ribs portion of "Mom's Crew Q." This recipe is great for entertaining because you can grill the ribs before your guests arrive and serve them right from the oven. You can figure that 1 rack of baby back ribs will feed 2 to 3 people depending on how much food is being served. When I grill ribs I like to use baby back, since they are tasty and everyone seems to love them. I will use this recipe to grill beef ribs also.

Suggested Listening:

Rib Joint
   Sam Price & His Texas Bluesicians
Soul Kitchen *The Doors*
Strikes Twice *Larry Carlton*
Ring of Fire *Dwight Yoakam*
A Question of Time *Depeche Mode*
Smokin' *Boston*
Got To Get You In To My Life
   The Beatles
My Old Flame *Duke Ellington*
Even Flow *Pearl Jam*
Take It To the Limit *The Eagles*
Goodbye Pork Pie Hat *Jeff Beck*
I Have the Touch *Peter Gabriel*
I Believe *Elmore James*
I Want To Take You Higher
   Ike & Tina Turner
1, 2, 3, 4 (Sumpin' New) *Coolio*
What Is and What Should Never Be
   Led Zeppelin

Smokin' Willie's Chicken

1 chicken cut into 8 pieces

Mom's BBQ Soak: (recipe page 91)

Smokin' Willie's Spice Rub

Smokin' Willie's Classic BBQ Sauce

Cut chicken into 8 pieces if whole (2 each; breasts, thighs, drumsticks, and wings). Wash chicken pieces. Soak chicken overnight in the refrigerator in Mom's BBQ Soak—you can soak for as little as a few hours or more, but it is better overnight! Remove chicken from soak and coat well with Smokin' Willie's Spice Rub. Place chicken directly over medium high heat. Stay close while searing over direct heat because you will get flare-ups from the fat in the skin. If you get a flare-up, just move the meat over the indirect part of the grill.

Sear and slow is the technique for this recipe. Sear both sides to get good color and to seal in juices, about 15 minutes, and then move over to indirect heat. Close lid and let cook for about 15 to 20 minutes and then turn over. Cook for another 15 or so minutes; do not open the lid more than you have to prevent losing heat and extending cooking time. Brush Smokin' Willie's Classic BBQ Sauce all over the chicken and close lid for 10 to 15 minutes. Serve hot and make sure you have plenty of napkins for this dish.

You can also finish cooking chicken in the oven. Remove chicken from grill and place in a roasting pan or foil tray and pour additional BBQ sauce over chicken. Seal the tray tightly with foil and put it in the oven at 250 degrees for 1 hour. This is great for parties and gatherings; you can grill ahead of time and bake it in the oven so you can spend time with your guests and not be at the grill. When you take chicken from the oven and remove the foil from the tray, the amazing aroma of BBQ will announce that dinner is served!

Serving Ideas: with BBQ baked beans, Smokin' Willie's potato salad, fresh green salad, and corn on the cob. This dish goes great with most anything!

Options: Fiesta BBQ Sauce & New Mexico Spice Rub for extra kick. Shanghai BBQ Sauce for an Asian influence.

30 minutes prep time
50 minutes on the grill
Baking optional

Barbeque chicken is as American as apple pie. There are as many ways to grill this bird as there are people that barbecue. This recipe is one part of the "Mom's Crew Q" menu, but it should also be recognized as a standalone recipe that has made many people happy at our "Qs." My good buddy Joe Teurlings and his family love this recipe. Joe is a beginning griller, and when he wants to impress his guests he cooks up the Smokin' Willie's Chicken. I have probably eaten this dish more than any other recipe in this book and I'm never tired of it!

Suggested Listening:

Chicken Strut *The Meters*
Dixie Chicken *Little Feat*
I'm Gonna Kill That Hen
   Blue Charlie
Soul Intro / The Chicken
   Jaco Pastorius
Oh Happy Day
   The Edwin Hawkins Singers
Birdland *Weather Report*
Blitzkrieg Bop (Hey Ho Let's Go!) *The Ramones*
Radar Love *Golden Earring*
Hip Hop Hooray
   Naughty By Nature
Wild Thing *The Troggs*
Smoke Gets In Your Eyes
   Roxy Music

Award-Winning Tri-Tip

One 3-pound Tri-Tip

2 tablespoons olive oil

3 tablespoons Smokin' Willie's Meat, Poultry & Seafood Spice Rub

Trim any fat or gristle from the Tri-Tip and then lightly rub all over with olive oil. Liberally sprinkle spice rub over the meat to completely coat with seasonings. Wrap with cellophane and store in the refrigerator overnight. Sprinkle some extra spice rub on the meat just before searing on the grill. Sear over high heat to create a crust, then flip and sear all sides, about 5 to 8 minutes a side. Move the Tri-Tip over indirect heat and close the lid for about 20 to 25 minutes. You do not have to worry about flare-ups while cooking over indirect heat, so do not open the lid unless you have to. Every time you lift the lid on the BBQ you lose heat, which extends your cooking time. After 20 to 25 minutes, lift the lid on the grill and gently turn the Tri-Tip over and close the lid for another 20 to 25 minutes or until cooked to your preference.

Remove the meat from the grill and put it under a foil tent and then let it rest for 10 minutes before slicing to help keep it juicy and tender.

Use Smokin' Willie's Classic BBQ sauce as an accompaniment. Slice the cooked Tri-Tip and coat with BBQ sauce to make fantastic sandwiches.

10 minutes prep
45 to 55 minutes grillin' time
10 minutes resting

This recipe won the first place Scovie Award for the Spice Rub Cook-Off at the 2007 Fiery Foods and BBQ Show in Albuquerque, New Mexico. BBQ cook-off champions will tell you that the secret to great BBQ is in the spice rub, and Smokin' Willie's Spice Rub is my secret ingredient. The Tri-Tip is well-known west of the Mississippi and originated in Santa Maria, California. This cut of meat is known as the sirloin tip and was made for grillin'. This recipe also happens to be one of my favorite dishes. Nearly everyone can enjoy this grilled Tri-Tip. I once helped grill 100 pounds of Tri-Tips for Aunt Tia Lupe's 80th birthday party at Camulos Ranch in Ventura County, California. I prepare the meat the day ahead of time so that the spices get absorbed in the meat, and this also makes a nice crust on the outside of the meat. This recipe travels well, to a friend's BBQ, picnic, or even camping.

Suggested Listening:

Rock & Roll *Led Zeppelin*
The Music Box *Genesis*
Cross Road Blues *Robert Johnson*
One Love *Bob Marley*
Higher Ground
  The Blind Boys Of Alabama
The Letter *Joe Cocker*
Red Hill Mining Town *U2*
Betcha By Golly, Wow *The Stylistics*
Roundabout *Yes*
All That You Dream *Little Feat*

Ahi Tuna Shanghai Style

4 ahi tuna filets (or any firm-textured fish, salmon works well)

2 tablespoons extra virgin olive oil

2 tablespoons lemon juice

Salt

Pepper

Smokin' Willie's Shanghai BBQ Sauce

Mix olive oil and lemon juice together. (I use a small Mason jar, seal it tight, and shake well!) Lightly coat tuna with olive oil/lemon mixture and lightly season with salt and pepper. Place tuna over high heat and cook for approximately 3 to 5 minutes to sear the outside. Turn over and brush with Smokin' Willie's Shanghai BBQ Sauce. Cook 3 to 5 minutes (about ¼ of the way). Turn over indirect heat and brush Shanghai BBQ Sauce over the top to create a glaze. The finished ahi tuna should be cooked 1/3 of the way on each side with the center 1/3 still pink. You can cook it longer for those who prefer their fish cooked more.

Serve and enjoy with white or brown rice, stir fry vegetables, Bicna's Pork Salad (page 26), and/or Shanghai Lettuce Wraps.

5 minutes to prep for the grill
10 minutes grill time

This recipe was conjured up while Chef Michael and I were working on the development of the Shanghai BBQ Sauce. It is so good that I can get kids who do not like fish to eat ahi tuna and like it!

I was doing a food demo at Whole Foods in Studio City—grilling on a BBQ outside and cooking Ahi Tuna with my Shanghai Sauce. A woman and her son were walking by and the young man, about 10 years old, made a comment about how good it smelled. His mother asked what I was sampling and I told her Ahi Tuna with my Shanghai BBQ sauce. She told her son and he said that he did not like fish but would be willing to give it a try. I gave him a small sample; he had one bite, smiled, and asked for more. I gave him a big piece of tuna and he told his mom that he liked this fish! They went back into the store and bought 2 bottles of the Smokin' Willie's Shanghai BBQ Sauce and some ahi tuna.

Suggested Listening:

Smoke On the Water *Deep Purple*
Changes in Attitude, Changes in Latitude *Jimmy Buffett*
Unchain My Heart *Ray Charles*
From the Sea *Dori Caymmi*
It's In the Way That You Use It *Eric Clapton*
A Question of Time *Depeche Mode*
Nobody But Me *The Human Beinz*
Get Down Tonight *K.C. & The Sunshine Band*
Acknowledgement (From A Love Supreme) *John Coletrane*
Wild World *Cat Stevens*
Sweet Little Angel *B.B. King*
Home By the Sea *Genesis*

BBQ Red Snapper

4 pounds red snapper or tilapia fillets or similar mild fish fillets

1 red bell pepper (seeded, not peeled, and cut into long ¼ inch strips)

1 yellow bell pepper (seeded, not peeled, and cut into long ¼ inch strips)

1 large red onion cut into ¼ inch rings

2 cloves of garlic, chopped

2 fresh limes (extra to squeeze over the tacos)

Salt

Pepper

Smokin' Willie's New Mexico Style Rub

Smokin' Willie's Classic BBQ Sauce (the Chipotle Sauce will overwhelm the fish)

Belizean Bar-B-Q Fish

Preheat oven to 350 degrees. Make a pan out of HEAVY DUTY aluminum foil to fit the fish in a single layer with some overlapping. Rinse, pat the fish dry, and lightly rub the fish fillets with Smokin' Willie's Rub on the top side only. Place fish in the foil "pan" and sprinkle on the garlic, then layer the red pepper, yellow pepper, and onion strips. Cut the limes in half and squeeze over the dish.

Pour Smokin' Willie's Classic BBQ Sauce in tablespoon quantities on top (approximately 1/2 cup). Seal all sides of the foil "pan" with another large piece of HEAVY DUTY foil. Overlap and roll the edges to seal and make this foil "lid" large enough so that it can expand during cooking. Place sealed packet on cookie sheet for support. Cook 30 minutes. Set packet on a large plate, peel back foil, and serve.

You can make this on the barbecue too, 15 to 25 minutes over hot coals.

Serve with a salad, beans, rice, and hot tortillas to make fantastic fish tacos.

15 minutes to prep for the grill
30 minutes grill time

My wife Diana's brothers Don and Kevin have been fans of my mom's BBQ sauce before there was a Smokin' Willie's. They have shared the sauce with friends and neighbors over the years. One of their neighbors, Judy Svendsen, shared this recipe with us at a gathering. It sounded great and after trying her recipe I asked if I could share it with you. Here is Judy's BBQ Red Snapper story and recipe!

"My family and I went to Belize for a vacation and while there, we hired a guide for an all-day fishing trip. We caught a number of red snapper and tilapia and around noon headed toward shore for a 'picnic' lunch. The family went off to explore the island, but I stayed to see how our guide prepared the fish for our lunch. Boy, was I glad that I did! When I returned home I made this dish with Smokin' Willie's BBQ Sauce, and my grandchildren said this was the best fish they had ever eaten."

Suggested Listening:

Fish (Shindelria Praematrus) *Yes*
Splish Splash *Bobby Darin*
Cabo Wabo *Van Halen*
Arc of a Diver *Steve Winwood*
Listen To Me *Bill Miller*
Because We Believe *Andrea Bocelli*
Jammin' *Bob Marley*
Milt Shake
  Dr. Jazz's Universal Remedy
Do It Again *The Beach Boys*
Some Kind of Wonderful
  Soul Brothers Six
Willin' *Little Feat*

Cruz's Kabobs

4 pounds Top Round beef (cut into 1 ½ to 2 inch cubes)

1 pound onions: pearl, red, and/or brown (or a mixture)

2 bell peppers: green, red, or yellow (or a mixture)

1 pound + mushrooms (get extra; they are the first to go & extra can be used in a salad)

1 pound cherry tomatoes

1 bottle Kraft Zesty Italian Salad Dressing

Metal or bamboo skewers

Options:

squash

zucchini

eggplant

Boil pearl onions for 5 to 7 minutes and remove outer skin. If you use yellow and/or red onions, cut them into wedges. Wash vegetables and cut bell peppers into 1 ½ to 2 inch squares (same with the onions). Clean the mushrooms and trim the stems so that the mushroom is flat. Cut your choice of meat into 1 ½ to 2 inch cubes. Mix all ingredients in a roasting or foil pan and coat well with salad dressing. Marinate overnight in the refrigerator. Soak bamboo skewers in water for ½ hour prior to assembling kabobs. Alternate between the meat and vegetables on the skewers; I start off with a mushroom, stem side facing away from you, then add meat, onion, meat, bell pepper, etc. I spear the tomatoes last. I try to put the same size pieces on the same skewers (larger pieces together, likewise smaller pieces together). The larger kabobs will be rarer and the smaller ones will be cooked more when you grill them for the same amount of time. Place kabobs in the roasting pan and pour the remaining dressing over the skewers. Grill over medium high heat for 5 to 7 minutes per side until done to your preference.

Mom's Time Saver: "I would get the London broil cut of beef when I would make the kabobs for a larger group of people. The London broil is just the right thickness to make uniform-sized cubes quick and easy."

1 hour and 15 minutes prep
25 to 35 minutes grilling time

My other mother, Cruz (Diana's beautiful mom), loved to cook. My fondest memories of Cruz are of her in the kitchen, cooking for the family. Diana comes from a large familia, seven brothers and two sisters, so Cruz did a lot of cooking and everything that I tasted was great. The only dish that Cruz would request for me to cook was her shish kabobs. This is another of my mom's older recipes. Mom told me this was actually my Grandma Launa Kelley's recipe. Grandma told my mom, "Because we have such a large family, this recipe could stretch out a roast and feed more people." Mom replied saying, "Launa was one hell of a cook."

Cruz's Kabobs is another recipe that can be made for larger groups by simply doubling or tripling the ingredients. All of the work is in the preparation—cutting the meat and vegetables into uniform size pieces. This will allow you to turn the kabobs so that they cook evenly. You can also make these kabobs with lamb, chicken, or pork. Cruz loved her kabobs and so will you!

Suggested Listening:

Rock the Casbah *The Clash*
Heaven *Boney James*
Stand By Me *The Blind Boys Of Alabama*
Every Hungry Woman *The Allman Brothers*
All My Loving *The Beatles*
Mambo No. 5 *Perez Prado & His Orchestra*
Knockin' On Heaven's Door
 Clapton, Guns N Roses, Bob Dylan
(Your Love Keeps Lifting Me) Higher and
 Higher *Jackie Wilson*
Body and Soul *Coleman Hawkins*
Besame Mucho *Andrea Bocelli*
This Could Be the Start Of Something Big
 Count Basie & His Orchestra
Cruz's Pick: Maggie May *Rod Stewart*
Mom's Pick: Sex Machine *James Brown*

Smokin' Fajitas

- 2 pounds skirt steak
- 1 red onion
- 1 bell pepper
- 4 cloves garlic minced
- Cilantro chopped (save some for garnish)
- ¼ cup olive oil
- ¼ cup liquid aminos/soy sauce
- ¼ cup red wine or red wine vinegar
- ¼ cup fresh lime or lemon juice
- 1 lime
- 2 to 3 tablespoons Smokin' Willie's New Mexico Spice Rub
- Salt
- Pepper
- 2 jalapeno peppers
- 1 Pasilla chile
- Fixin's:
- 1 dozen flour tortillas
- Sour cream
- Shredded cheese
- 1 large tomato, chopped
- Grilled salsa
- Guacamole

Mix together in a bowl with a whisk the oil, soy sauce, wine, juice of 3 to 4 limes, New Mexico Spice Rub, minced garlic, fresh cracked pepper, and a pinch of salt. Set aside. Wash the bell peppers and chiles if you are going to use them to make the fajitas hotter. Core and seed peppers and slice into strips, about ½ inch wide. Remove the skin from the onions and quarter. Remove any gristle or membrane from the skirt steak and then place steak, onion, peppers, and 3 tablespoons of cilantro in a gallon Ziploc® bag or glass casserole dish. Whisk marinade and pour over meat and veggies. Seal by removing as much air as possible or cover with Saran™ wrap and refrigerate overnight. Anticipation builds with this dish as you wait for the next day to grill the fajitas.

Take fajitas out of the fridge ½ hour before cooking them. Reserving some of the marinade (measuring cup works great), put everything on the grill over medium high heat, 8 to 10 minutes, depending on the heat and the thickness of the meat. Turn over halfway through cooking and pour some of the reserved marinade on top, cooking for another 8 to 10 minutes or until medium-rare. Let rest for a couple of minutes and then cut the steak against the grain into thin strips. Squeeze fresh juice from lime wedges just before serving, as the aroma and taste is fantastic.

Heat tortillas on the grill or on the stove top; use a dish towel on a dinner plate to cover and keep the heated tortillas warm. Serve while sizzling hot with any or all of the fixin's. Use corn tortillas to create fajita tacos!

30 minutes cutting and prepping
15 to 20 minutes on the grill

Here is a tasty Southwestern recipe that you can cook at home that is just as good as you can get at any restaurant, if not better. The secret is in the Smokin' Willie's New Mexico Spice Rub that gives this recipe a mouth-watering savory flavor. This recipe will be even better if you use red wine—one that you would drink! We have been favoring a Merlot lately, but use your favorite. I use a ½ cup of wine when I make this dish. I prefer lime juice for the marinade instead of lemon, but try them both and see which one you prefer.

Fajitas originated in Texas, at least that is what Texans have been telling me! The original fajitas recipe calls for skirt steak, but they have evolved with the times and we now have chicken and seafood fajitas. Flank steak can be substituted for skirt steak, or you can use boneless, skinless chicken breasts and thighs as well as shrimp. (I would marinate the chicken for a shorter period of time, 2 to 6 hours.) On the grill, stove, or even a cast iron Dutch oven on top of wood coals at your campsite, this is a fun recipe that everyone will love. I usually grill my fajitas but I have cooked them on the stove on rare occasions. I have a cast iron fajitas skillet, but I like to use my grandmother's cast iron skillet to keep them sizzling hot. I recommend that you use mesquite wood, charcoal, or chips when grilling the fajitas; it gives it an original smoky Southwestern flavor.

Suggested Listening:

Oye Como Va *Santana*
La Grange *ZZ Top*
Boot Scootin' Boogie *Brooks & Dunn*
The Unforgiven *Metallica*
Whole Lot of Love *Led Zeppelin*
That'll Be the Day *Linda Ronstadt*
Peace *Malo*
Southern Man *Neil Young*
Shake Your Rump To the Funk *The Barkays*
Sent For You Yesterday and Here You Come Today *Count Basie & His Orchestra*

Devin's Kielbasa

1 to 2 pounds kielbasa or smoked sausage

¾ cup Smokin' Willie's Classic BBQ Sauce

Kielbasa on the Grill

Slice the kielbasa into ½ to 1 inch pieces. Grill over medium heat. If using charcoal you will want to lower the charcoal because the fat will drip on to the coals and cause flare-ups. Grill until browned on one side, about 3 to 5 minutes, then turn over with tongs. Once both sides are grilled, put the sausage in a covered oven-proof pot or in a covered foil tray. Lather with Smokin' Willie's Classic BBQ Sauce to taste and serve right away, or put in the oven so that you can serve them later. Now, wasn't this a hard recipe?

5 minutes to cut kielbasa
10 to 15 minutes grilling time

4 to 5 pounds kielbasa or smoked sausage

1 bottle Smokin' Willie's Classic BBQ Sauce

Kielbasa for a Crowd

Preheat oven to 375°. Slice kielbasa into ½ to 1 inch pieces. Place in an oven-proof pot, cover, and place in the oven for 35 to 45 minutes. With heat-proof mitts or pot holders, CAREFULLY pour fat from the pot of kielbasa into a heat resistant bowl. Carefully pour kielbasa in a Crock-Pot/slow cooker or use the same pot and cover with Smokin' Willie's Classic BBQ Sauce (½ to ¾ of the bottle or more to taste). Set the Crock-Pot/slow cooker on high heat for about 20 minutes; then adjust to the low setting. You can let the kielbasa simmer for hours in this manner. The longer the kielbasa slowly cooks in the Crock-Pot the better it gets! I have had the kielbasa on a low temperature setting for over 8 hours.

A word of warning: Kielbasa is always the first thing consumed. When your guests arrive, the smell of the kielbasa simmering in Smokin' Willie's Classic BBQ Sauce will drive them nuts. I like to make this dish first when I do "Mom's Crew Q" menu so I do not have to cook them on the grill; this also saves me time towards the end of cooking the Crew Q.

10 minutes cutting the kielbasa
45 minutes in the oven
1 to 8 hours in a Crock-Pot

This is the easiest and most requested recipe that I make. Try it and you will see why everybody loves it. When I make "Mom's Crew Q," it is the first thing that runs out. Kielbasa is a cooked Polish sausage; Mom always used Hillshire Farms brand, but you can use any smoked sausage or kielbasa.

Our nephew Devin is always asking for this dish when he comes over to our house. One time we were having a big family gathering, but there wasn't enough kielbasa to make it by the time Devin arrived with his family. Devin was bummed, almost to the point of tears, and I did not have any left in the fridge (I almost always have a pack of kielbasa in the refrigerator for emergencies). So I ran to the store and picked up a package just for Devin. Every time I cook this recipe, I think of him!

This is also a great potluck or Super Bowl party dish using the oven method. We get invited to our close friends, the Razo's family Super Bowl party, and I kid you not, they have at least five TVs going in different rooms of the house. I used to think I was invited because of my bubbly personality, but I think the truth is more like Diana is the one with the personality and I am the one with the kielbasa.

You can cook kielbasa two different ways: on the grill (for smaller amounts) or in the oven (for big gatherings), so here you have it!

Suggested Listening:

Turn It On, Turn It Up, Turn Me Loose
   Dwight Yoakam
Heart of Gold *Neil Young*
Everybody Have Fun Tonight *Wang Chung*
You Really Got Me *Van Halen*
You're Still a Young Man *Tower Of Power*
The "In" Crowd *Ramsey Louis Trio*
Wooly Bully *Sam The Sham & The Pharaohs*
Our House *Madness*
Well, Git It! *Tommy Dorsey & His Orchestra*
Pride and Joy
   Stevie Ray Vaughan & Double Trouble
Sunshine and Summertime *Faith Hill*
Ride of the Valkyries *Wagner*
Party at Ground Zero *Fishbone*

Dad's Steak

1 boneless steak of your choice per person

High quality extra virgin olive oil

Smokin' Willie's Spice Rub

Salt

Pepper

Lightly coat steaks with olive oil and shake Smokin' Willie's Rub on the steak and coat to taste. Pat or rub into steak. I put quite a bit on my steaks because I like the crust it produces. You can do this the night before—just wrap in cellophane, Ziploc® bag, or vacuum-pack with a Foodsaver.

Grill over medium high heat, 4 to 5 minutes over direct heat then turn over direct heat for another 4 to 6 minutes or until desired degree of doneness, depending on the heat and the thickness of the steaks. Let the steaks rest under a foil tent for 5 to 10 minutes so that you do not lose all of those precious juices.

Serve with baked potatoes, fresh garden salad, and bread grilled with the garlic bread spread (page 42), for a meal fit for a king! Microwave Smokin' Willie's BBQ sauce on the side for use as a steak sauce, but with these seasonings your steak will be delicious all on its own.

10 minutes prep the night before
10 to 15 minutes on the grill

This quick and easy recipe is for steaks that do not have a bone in them. This one reminds me of my dad. He could grill a mean steak! When I was in the Boy Scouts Troop 77, we did a lot of camping & hiking and this is when my dad started showing me how to grill. As I recall my youth, the kids would have hot dogs or hamburgers and the adults would have steak; Dad knew how to please everyone with his grilling!

Here is a great reason to get to know your local butcher: they will show you what to look for in a good cut of meat and make sure you get the best cuts. I look for clean marbling of the meat; thin streaks of fat evenly mixed throughout the meat. I pick the thickness so that the steaks will finish at the same time, grilled to the desired degree of cooking. Rare steaks will be thicker and the well-cooked steaks should be thinner. New York Strip, rib-eyes, or filet mignons, whichever is your favorite, here is a surefire method to grill an amazing steak, just like dear ol' Dad.

Suggested Listening:

Sweet Soul Music *Arthur Conley*
My Father's Eyes *Eric Clapton*
Pump It Up *Elvis Costello*
Minute By Minute *The Doobie Brothers*
Cattle Call *Emmylou Harris*
Red House *Jimi Hendrix*
Got To Have It *Willie Mason*
In the Mood *Glenn Miller*
It's Your Thing *The Isley Brothers*
Straight, No Chaser *Thelonious Monk*
Jump Around *House Of Pain*

Shanghai Chicken on a Stick

2 to 3 boneless/skinless chicken breasts

Salt

Pepper

¼ cup Smokin' Willie's Shanghai BBQ Sauce

8 to 12 skewers, depending on the amount of chicken

If you use bamboo skewers, soak in water for 15 to 30 minutes before using.

Wash chicken & pat dry. Slice chicken breasts lengthwise into ¼ inch thick strips. Marinade chicken strips in Smokin' Willie's Shanghai Sauce for a few hours. Thread chicken on skewers and pour the remaining sauce over the top of the skewered chicken. Grill over medium heat for about 7 to 10 minutes and then turn over until done 7 to 10 minutes. Brush on extra Shanghai sauce if desired.

Options: fish, beef, pork, shrimp to be threaded on skewers, a la Thai Satay.

Try Classic or Fiesta BBQ Sauce for a different flavor.

Serving Ideas: white or brown rice, stuffed shiitake mushrooms, BBQ pork salad, chicken lettuce wraps, and/or stir fry vegetables. To use Smokin' Willie's Shanghai BBQ sauce as a dipping sauce, microwave in a small microwavable bowl for 25 to 30 seconds. Then you can use this as a dip for egg rolls or pot stickers to accompany this meal.

20 minutes prep
7 to 10 minutes grilling time

Shanghai Chicken on a Stick is our Sister Olivia's favorite recipe. She doesn't have a BBQ so she often cooks it on the stove. This dish is so tasty and easy to make that this recipe will become a favorite in your household. I only use thin cuts of meat to marinate in sauces that have sugar in them because they cook quickly and are less likely to burn on the grill. A medium heat and a short cooking time will work well with this recipe. This Shanghai Chicken on a Stick is grilled like Thai Satay, but with a different flavor altogether. This recipe is mobile so you can grill it at the park or bring it to a friend's house. I have an electric George Foreman Grill that I use to cook this recipe when I do food demos.

Suggested Listening:

One Night In Bangkok *Murray Head*
Good Vibrations
 Markey Mark & The Funky Bunch
Louie, Louie *The Kingsmen*
I Walk the Line *Johnny Cash*
Whatcha See Is Whatcha Get
 The Dramatics
Stand By Me *Ben E. King*
Little Red Corvette *Prince*
Mack the Knife *Bobby Darin*
Take Five *The Dave Brubeck Quartet*
West End Blues *Louis Armstrong*

Asian Chicken Kabobs

2 pounds chicken breasts (boneless/skinless)

Pineapple (fresh or 1 can of rings)

2 bell peppers

1 red onion

Smokin' Willie's Shanghai BBQ Sauce

1 tablespoon sesame seeds (optional)

Bamboo skewers (soak in water for 15 to 30 minutes before using)

Cut chicken breasts into 1½ to 2 inch pieces and place in a gallon baggie or Tupperware®. Cut bell peppers and onion into same size pieces as the chicken and add to chicken. Slice individual pineapple rings into 4 or 5 pieces that are big enough to put on a skewer and add to chicken mixture along with enough Shanghai BBQ Sauce to coat well. Marinate at least 2 hours and as long as overnight. Soak the bamboo skewers in water for at least a half hour before you put together the kabobs. Alternate bell peppers, onion, chicken, and pineapple as you put them on the skewers. Cook over medium high heat for about 7 to 10 minutes a side until the chicken is cooked through. Brush some Shanghai BBQ sauce over the kabobs towards the end of grilling.

For a lighter flavor you can use all of the ingredients without marinating them and brush the Shanghai BBQ sauce on the kabobs while they are on the grill over indirect heat.

Options: Shrimp, Beef, Pork

Serve with brown or white rice, egg rolls, vegetable stir fry, BBQ Stuffed Shiitake Mushrooms (page 12), and/or Bicna's Pork Salad (page 26).

20 minutes to prep
7 to 10 minutes on the grill

Made with chicken, pineapple, sweet peppers, and red onion, coated with Smokin' Willie's Shanghai BBQ Sauce and served over a bed of rice, this is a meal fit for royalty. The recipe can be prepared ahead of time or at the last minute, and you can marinate with the BBQ sauce for a richer, deeper flavor or lightly brush on the sauce for more of a "highlight" taste. You can use canned pineapple rings and cut the rings into 4 or 5 wedges, but I like to use fresh pineapple when I make this meal, and I grill the leftover pineapple rings for dessert (page 99). This tasty dish is easy, healthy, and cooks quickly. It's a grillin' must-have!

Suggested Listening:

Bring It On *Seal*
Catching the Sun *Spyro Gyra*
Ooh Baby, Baby
    Smokey Robinson & The Miracles
Wild Wild Life *Talking Heads*
Desire *U2*
Sailing *Christopher Cross*
That'll Be the Day
    Buddy Holly & The Crickets
Boom Boom *John Lee Hooker*
Solitude *Billie Holiday*

Matt's Grilled Tofu

1 package extra firm tofu
(Matt likes garlic and pepper tofu)

Smokin' Willie's Shanghai BBQ Sauce

Open the package of tofu and drain liquid. Slice tofu squares down the middle to make thinner tofu steaks/squares. Lightly wipe the grill with olive oil on a paper towel using tongs. Over medium heat, grill one side of tofu over direct heat for 7 to 10 minutes to get nice sear marks. Flip over with a spatula and grill the other side 7 to 10 minutes. Move over indirect heat and brush Smokin' Willie's Shanghai BBQ Sauce on both sides. Serve hot off the grill. I will drizzle extra sauce on top when I serve them.

I serve this recipe at home over a bed of brown or white rice, steamed vegetables, or use the grilled tofu in a stir fry. This recipe travels well and can be reheated later.

5 minutes prep
20 minutes grill time

My son Matt was a vegetarian at the time and he asked me to BBQ something besides vegetables & veggie burgers, so we tried tofu. While the Classic Sauce & Fiesta Sauce is good on Tofu, the Shanghai sauce is the hands-down favorite. This recipe is simple and quick and is a change of pace on the grill. I have even had people who avoid tofu tell me that this recipe tastes great. Try it, you'll like it!

Suggested Listening:

Sing Your Life *Morrissey*
Where Have All the Cowboys Gone
　Paula Cole
Strawberry Fields Forever
　The Beatles
Can't Find My Way Home
　Blind Faith
Red Rain
　Peter Gabriel
New York, New York
　Frank Sinatra
Attitude *The Misfits*
My Generation *The Who*
Never Too Far *Bill Miller*

Smokin' Willie's Meatloaf

2 pounds ground meat; beef, turkey, chicken, or even bison

2 large carrots

3 stocks of celery

1 small onion

2 tablespoons Smokin' Willie's Spice Rub

¾ cup saltine cracker crumbs or bread crumbs

¾ cup Smokin' Willie's Classic BBQ Sauce

2 eggs

2 loaf pans
(I use foil for ease of cleaning so I don't have to clean the pan)

Dice carrots, celery, and onion into small pieces. Mix eggs & BBQ Sauce in a bowl before adding to the other ingredients. Incorporate all ingredients in a large mixing bowl by hand (kids love to do this). Divide in half and put into the loaf pans. Top with BBQ sauce. Cover with foil and bake at 350 degrees for 45 minutes. Remove foil cover after 45 minutes and cook 15 minutes longer uncovered until done. Let meatloaf rest, covered, for about 10 minutes and serve.

Serve with mashed potatoes and gravy, corn, crisp salad, and a tasty French roll.

Variations:

Spicy Meatloaf: Fiesta with Chipotle BBQ Sauce & New Mexico Spice Rub

Shanghai Meatloaf: Shanghai BBQ Sauce (use salt and pepper instead of Smokin' Willie's Spice Rub). Other ingredient options are green onion, bok choy, water chestnuts, and anything that sounds good to you.

Experiment and make this boring, everyday dish one that your family will look forward to.

20 minutes prep
1 hour cooking time

This recipe comes from a fan of Smokin' Willie's. I was doing a demo in a Whole Foods Market when a woman said, "This BBQ sauce would make a great meatloaf!" I tried it, and she was right on the mark. Now I get people telling me that they tried it and this is the only way they will make meatloaf. I will warn you that I also got one complaint: "There was not enough left over for sandwiches." So this recipe is for two loaves. You can freeze one for later, but if there are four or more in your household, you had better cook both.

Suggested Listening:

Paradise At the Dashboard Light
  Meatloaf
Can't Get Enough *Bad Company*
Carried Away *Crosby, Stills and Nash*
Respect *Aretha Franklin*
Sweet Child of Mine
  Guns N' Roses
Bring It on Home
  Sonny Boy Williamson
Come On In My Kitchen
  Robert Johnson
Bad To the Bone
  George Thorogood & The Destroyers
I Heard It Through the Grapevine
  Gladys Knight & The Pips
Feats Don't Fail Me Now *Little Feat*

group fixin's

Camping

Breakfast Burritos

Dad's Grilled Steak

Dad's Camping Chicken

Kielbasa

Shrimp on a Stick

Teriyaki Sandwiches

Smokin' Chicken

Cruz's Kabobs

Fajitas

Hamburgers / Hot Dogs

Matt's Tofu

Guida's Quesadillas

Potato Salad

Mom's Baked Beans

Grilled Stuffed Apples & Pears

Fruit Kabobs

This is where I started learning the art of grillin'—with my family, the Boy Scouts, and then on my own when I started driving. Coals from a wood fire to a propane camping stove, I learned from my dad, mom, and scout leaders. Camping with my family in Bouquet Canyon to backpacking in the high Sierras and even pulling over by the side of Highway 1 in my van with a view of the Pacific Ocean—food just tastes better cooked outdoors (the smell is enhanced also!). I like to eat, so I started learning to cook at an early age. Camping and picnicking require planning your meals ahead of time, with attention paid to ease of cooking and cleanup. I often make meals ahead of time at home and then freeze them for use on camping trips. I can use the frozen food instead of ice in my cooler and then grill the food as it thaws. I believe you can eat with style and flavor when you are camping or at the park for a family picnic. Here is a list of recipes in this book that have been used when I have been camping in the great outdoors:

Suggested Listening:

Sleeping Bag *ZZ Top*
Family Affair *Sly And The Family Stone*
Heart of the Sunrise *Yes*
The Hunter *Albert King*
Woodchoppers Ball *Woody Herman*
Fire & Rain *James Taylor*
Moon Dreams *Miles Davis*
Down By the River Bed *Los Lobos*
Ramblin' Man *The Allman Brothers*
Three Observations of One Ocean
  William Ackerman
Summertime Blues *Eddie Cochran*

Breakfast Burritos

12 eggs

12 tortillas

1 pound shredded cheese

2 pounds Chorizo (or sausage)

1 package frozen Potatoes O'Brien

Salsa (grilled, page 15)

Foil

Options:
Rice
Beans
Bell Pepper
Onions
Bacon
Ham diced
Hash Brown Potatoes
Hot Sauce

You will need two skillets for this recipe. Start cooking the frozen Potatoes O'Brien in one skillet and the Chorizo or sausage in the other. Scramble the eggs in a bowl and set aside. Drain any grease from the cooked sausage and slowly add the scrambled egg, cooking eggs and sausage together. Tear off a length of foil, enough to wrap the burrito that you are making, and place a heated tortilla in the center. On the tortilla sprinkle cheese, then egg/sausage mixture, potatoes, and salsa (for those who like it spicy). Wrap the tortilla into a burrito and then wrap with the foil. Make and wrap with foil each burrito individually; this makes it easy to cook and eat. Do not forget to mark them as you are making them. Place in the freezer for at least 48 hours.

45 minutes to make a dozen burritos
10 to 15 minutes to heat over the coals

Here is a recipe I make for breakfast during our camping trips. Eggs are great to eat when you are camping, but a real pain to clean up. With this recipe there is no cleanup necessary. Made ahead of time, wrapped in foil, the burritos are frozen and act as ice in the cooler and they usually thaw out by the next morning. Cooked over the hot coals of the morning fire or on a skillet on the camp stove, everybody loves this breakfast, and not just when you are camping! This seems to be a constant theme for this book, but you can customize this recipe to the tastes of you, your family, and friends.

Chorizo is a spicy Mexican style sausage that I use most of the time for this recipe, but you can use bacon or sausage. Have a magic marker handy when you put these burritos together so you can label the foil. I customize the burritos to order; some like it spicy and some do not, and then I write the person's name on the foil. These burritos offer a hearty breakfast in a pinch, and not just for camping. Just place frozen burrito in the microwave for a few minutes (without the foil) and you have a hot breakfast to go. I try to keep some stashed in the freezer, but they do not seem to last very long. Make more than you think; everyone seems to be hungrier when you are camping and we don't want anybody to go hungry. This is my classic recipe that will make a dozen burritos.

Suggested Listening:

Can't You See *Marshall Tucker Band*
Further On Up the Road *Eric Clapton*
Here Comes the Sun *The Beatles*
Waiting for the Sun *The Doors*
Just Another Day *Oingo Boingo*
Sitting On Top of the World *Howlin' Wolf*
Ain't No Mountain High Enough *Diana Ross*
Go Fishing *Roger Waters*
The Sun Is Shinning *The Yardbirds*
Two Old Sidewinders *Waylon & Willie*

Dad's Camping Chicken

1 chicken whole or two halves
feeds 4 to 5

Barbeque Soak
(page 91)

1 tablespoon or more Smokin' Willie's Spice Rub

1 bottle Smokin' Willie's Classic BBQ Sauce
(take with you to the campsite)

Wash chicken and cut in half; this is where good poultry shears come in handy and makes cutting chicken easy. Marinate chicken in barbeque soak recipe overnight. After chicken has marinated, remove from the soak, sprinkle with Smokin' Willie's Spice Rub, and freeze in plastic bags. Dad would place the frozen chicken in the cooler where it would act as ice and thaw out so that you can grill it the next night. Grill over medium high heat starting with the cut side down first. Grill for about 20 to 25 minutes, and then turn over for another 20 to 25 minutes or until cooked through. Keep an eye on the chicken while it is on the grill because of flare-ups (good time for a couple of beers!). Brush on Smokin' Willie's Classic BBQ sauce at the very end so that the BBQ sauce does not burn. Serve hot and enjoy! Make sure you have lots of napkins for this recipe.

Options: Spicy chicken using Smokin' Willie's New Mexico Spice Rub and Fiesta with Chipotle BBQ Sauce

Dad would serve his grilled chicken with corn on the cob and potato salad. Baked potato, green salad, potato chips, carrots, and celery sticks are other good options that are easy to prepare ahead of time to make your camping trip a gourmet experience.

20 minutes chicken prep
45 to 55 minutes grillin' at the campsite

The only chicken my dad would take camping would be this simple recipe. He loved to make our mouths water with the smell of BBQ chicken while we were camping. Everyone else would be cooking hamburgers and hot dogs while my dad grilled half chickens, slathering on Mom's BBQ sauce. Campsites usually have BBQ grates that are wider apart than the ones you would use at home, so Dad liked to use half chickens, so that smaller pieces would not fall through the grill slats and into the coals. All the preparation was done at home beforehand so that all Dad had to do was get the fire started and grill the chicken. Dad would figure that ½ chicken would feed two people. Mom would get whole chickens and cut them in half, but you can buy half chickens from the store or butcher. We would usually enjoy with corn on the cob wrapped in foil (page 39) or sometimes baked potatoes (page 37). We would always bring foil when we would go camping to wrap any leftovers, but leftovers are doubtful as it seems I can always eat more when I am camping. One thing my mom and dad made sure of was that when we went camping, we would eat like royalty and you can too!

Suggested Listening:

In My Life *The Beatles*
People Get Ready *Jeff Beck with Rod Stewart*
Give Me the Night *George Benson*
One Bourbon, One Scotch, One Beer
  John Lee Hooker
Compared To What
  Les McCann & Eddie Harris
Dance To the Music *Sly & The Family Stone*
Ain't That A Shame *Fats Domino*
Hold On, I'm Comin' *Sam & Dave*
Strangers In the Night *Frank Sinatra*
Do Your Thing
  Charles Wright and the 103rd St Band

Mom's Crew Q

Chicken

Ribs

Kielbasa Sausage

Smokin' Willie's Classic, Fiesta, or Shanghai BBQ Sauce

Smokin' Willie's Crew Q/Grillin' For A Crowd or Party
The night before the gathering remove the membrane from the back of the ribs. Cut a rack of baby back ribs in half or thirds, beef individually; this makes it easier to turn on the grill, cooks faster, and allows for more sauce cooked on the ends. Cut the whole chicken into 8 pieces. Soak the ribs and chicken separately in the Smokin' Willie's soak overnight. You can also cut kielbasa into ½ to 1 inch pieces and store in a Ziploc® bag.

Start early and finish the Q in the oven so you can enjoy time with your guests. For a 1:00 PM party time start the BBQ at about 9:00 or 9:30 AM.

½ hour before you start the BBQ, soak 1 cup of the flavored wood chips of your choice in water (if you are going to use them, which I recommend). Take the meat from soak and sprinkle spice rub on ribs and chicken. Start off with the ribs, sear for color (10 to 15 minutes) and finish on indirect heat (35 to 45 minutes). During the last 10 minutes brush with Smokin Willie's Classic, Fiesta, or Shanghai BBQ Sauce. Put grilled ribs in an oven-proof roasting pan or large foil pan, seal with foil, and place them in the oven. Do not overcook on the grill because you will finish the cooking process in the oven. Grill the chicken in the same manner as the ribs, and then put the chicken in a tray, seal with foil, and then put in the oven. Put the cooked ribs, chicken, and kielbasa in the same enamel roasting pan in the oven and serve buffet style right out of the pan.

Bake ribs & chicken in the oven to finish cooking and then you have time to get ready for your guests:

Finish with the kielbasa. The coals will be cooler, with less flair-ups.

Option: Cut and cook kielbasa in an oven-proof pan with a lid at 375 for 40 to 45 minutes. Drain liquid into a heat-proof measuring cup. Put kielbasa into a slow cooker/Crock-Pot. Do this early and your crew will have something to munch on right away and you will not have to cook the kielbasa on the grill.

Mom almost always serves her baked beans and a fresh garden salad. Dessert would most likely be the Bonus Recipe (page 106).

1 hour prep
1 hour to grill
Finish off in the oven

This is my mom's "Q for a Crew" chicken, ribs, and kielbasa menu for a large group that she has cooked for as many years as I can remember. Mom is a big racing fan, especially stock cars, and my brother Brian has been racing since 1988. Mom used to can her BBQ sauce in mason jars to help sponsor Brian's car. She would cook up this amazing menu of BBQ to feed everyone who supported Brian's race team. After Mom started feeding the pit crew with her Q, it seems that Brian did not have any problem getting volunteers to help out with the car!

Read the recipes for ribs (page 60), BBQ chicken (page 62), and kielbasa (page 74) when you grill this menu for the first time for additional cooking tips.

Whenever there was a big family gathering, the Crew Q was always requested. The ribs, chicken, and sausage combo is a hit every time!

Oven Temperature & Time
350 for 30 to 45 minutes
325 up to an hour
300 1 ½ hours
250 2 hours
200 2 + hours

Suggested Listening:

Fire *Jimi Hendrix*
Pink Cadillac *Aretha Franklin*
Fast Car *Tracy Chapman*
Back Yard Ritual *Miles Davis*
Supper's Ready *Genesis*
People Get Ready
  The Blind Boys Of Alabama
Come Together *The Beatles*
Good Times Roll *The Cars*
Route 66 *Nat "King" Cole*
In My Blood *Larry Carlton*
Concrete Jungle *Bob Marley*
I Can Hear Music *The Beach Boys*

Smokin' Willie's BBQ Turkey

One 10- to 15-pound defrosted natural turkey
(no water or salt injected or added)

Smokin' Fowl Soak
(recipe page 90)

Olive oil

Salt

Fresh cracked pepper

Smokin' Willie's New Mexico Spice Rub

Follow the soak recipe the night before to prepare the turkey for the rotisserie. Remove turkey from the soak and pat dry. Lightly coat turkey with olive oil and season inside and out with salt, pepper, and Smokin' Willie's New Mexico Spice Rub.

Carefully mount turkey on to the rotisserie spit making sure that it is balanced. Use cooking string soaked in water to tie off the wings and legs so that they are not hanging from the turkey as it rotates on the rotisserie. Do not stuff the turkey when you grill because it will cook faster and more evenly than if you stuff it, but you can put aromatics (such as onion, celery, rosemary, etc) inside the cavity of the turkey if you like. Cook over medium high heat. This can take 2½ to 3½ hours or longer depending on the size of the bird and the heat of the BBQ. If you are using a charcoal grill, you will have to add more charcoal during the cooking process. Try not to open the lid to the BBQ too many times; every time you open the lid you lose heat. Cook until thermometer reads 180 degrees measured from the inside of the thigh without touching bone. Carefully remove turkey from the BBQ on the spit. You should have help and use cooking mitts so that you do not burn yourself or drop the turkey. Remove from spit and cover with a foil tent. Let rest for 20 to 30 minutes depending on the size of the turkey. Carve and serve this beautiful turkey for a unique holiday treat!

Serve this dish with wild rice stuffing, mashed potatoes and gravy, a vegetable, salad, bread, and your favorite holiday dessert.

Try this recipe first with a good-sized chicken or small turkey if you are not used to cooking with the rotisserie on the BBQ. This will build up your confidence and help to insure success when you try this recipe for the big dinner.

20 minutes prep
overnight soak
2 1/2 to 4 hours on the rotisserie
30 minutes resting time

Here is a unique and tasty way to serve your Thanksgiving turkey with a great Southwestern flavor. This recipe is also a delicious way to enjoy turkey all year long, not just during the holidays. When you use a rotisserie on your BBQ, all you have to do is keep an eye on the temperature as the turkey is pretty much self-basting. When you BBQ a turkey, make sure you have a heavy-duty rotisserie rated to handle the weight of your turkey. This recipe can burn out a rotisserie if you overload it. When you are shopping for your turkey, look for all natural, not processed where they inject salt and water. I have cooked many birds on the grill and it is always better tasting and juicer when they are given a soaking overnight. This is one of the harder recipes in my book, but I think it is just a little more work than roasting a turkey in the oven, and this is a great change of pace for the holidays or any time of the year.

Suggested Listening:

Holiday *Madonna*
Fine and Mellow *Billie Holiday*
Hungry Heart
  Bruce Springsteen & the E Street Band
Let the Good Times Roll
  Bobby Bland and B.B. King
Backfield In Motion *Mel and Tim*
It's a Family Affair
  Sly and the Family Stone
Change *Tears for Fears*
U Can't Touch This *M.C. Hammer*
Compared To What
  Les McCann and Eddie Harris
Free Bird *Lynyrd Skynard*
What's Going On *Marvin Gaye*
Comin' Home *Deep Purple*
Our House
  Crosby, Stills, Nash and Young
Les Feuilles Mortes (Autumn Leaves)
  Andrea Bocelli

marinades
sauces
butters

Smokin' Fowl Soak for BBQ Turkey

2 cups kosher salt or 1 cup of regular salt

½ cup brown sugar

¼ cup Smokin' Willie's New Mexico Spice Rub

1 tablespoon black peppercorns

4 to 6 bay leaves

2 lemons, squeezed

½ cup apple cider vinegar

¼ cup liquid smoke

2 gallons iced water

Combine salt, sugar, spice rub, black peppercorns, and bay leaves in a pan with 2 cups of water and bring to a boil. Stir to mix the ingredients and remove from heat until the mixture is room temperature. Refrigerate until completely chilled.

Mix all of the ingredients in a clean 5-gallon bucket with a lid. (I brought my ice chest with me to the store to make sure that the plastic bucket fit so I could brine the turkey overnight in the ice chest packed with ice to make room in my refrigerator. There never seems to be enough room in the fridge when I cook a holiday dinner.)

Wash turkey inside and out with cold water. Place turkey breast side down in the bucket with the soak in it and shake to make sure that there are no air pockets in the turkey. Cover and place in the refrigerator or in an ice chest and cover with ice.

20 minutes prep work
Soak overnight

Suggested Listening:

Chasin' the Bird *Charlie Parker*
What I Like About You
  The Romantics
Boogie Chillin' *John Lee Hooker*
Let's Get It On *Marvin Gaye*
I Got Love If You Want It *Slim Harpo*
Some Kind of Wonderful
  Soul Brothers Six
Funky Attitude *Sheila E.*
Smoke Along the Track
  Emmylou Harris
Dirty Deeds Done Dirt Cheap
  AC/DC
Where Did Our Love Go
  Diana Ross & The Supremes

BBQ Soak

1½ cups vinegar

¼ cup liquid smoke

½ cup lemon juice

3 tablespoons salt

2 tablespoons pepper

2 tablespoons Smokin' Willie's Spice Rub

2 tablespoons garlic powder

1 tablespoon onion powder

2 bay leaves

Water to cover the meat

Wash the meat with water and put in an acid-proof container; do not use aluminum. I use a big plastic Tupperware® with a snap-on lid; Mom uses an old roasting pan that she covers with foil. Mix all of the ingredients together and pour over the meat. Add water until the meat is covered.

Refrigerate overnight. Just before you are going to start cooking, take the meat out of the soak, sprinkle the meat with Smokin' Willie's spice rub, and put it on the grill (make sure that you do not use the leftover soak to brush on the meat that is on the grill because of contamination between raw and cooked meat).

You can adjust the measurements to fit the amount of meat that you are cooking. Remember, this is not a strong tasting soak but you can make it stronger for shorter soaking times. This soak also helps you prepare your grillin' for parties and larger groups (see Mom's Crew Q recipe). Try other herbs and spices to give your food your own signature!

10 minutes prep work
Soak overnight

Mom has used this soak (BBQ lingo for a marinade or brine) for as long as I can remember. It is her grilling secret for ribs, chicken, and pork chops—besides the sauce, that is! Barbeque purists would laugh at this recipe and say that this is not the way to barbeque, but these days most of us do not have the time to spend hours barbequing. Try grilling with and without the soak and see for yourself the benefits of the savory flavor when using this recipe. I, myself, use this soak all the time. This is a recipe that is to be used overnight, but it can also be used for shorter periods of time; just add more seasonings and salt. You need to soak for at least two hours to achieve any benefit, but you will want to soak the meat overnight to achieve full flavor (it's worth the effort). If you do not have enough time to soak, no worries—just add more spice rub before you put the meat on the grill.

It is hard to give you measurements for this recipe because of all the variables. How much meat, how long you are going to soak … so you can experiment and customize this recipe to your family's tastes.

Suggested Listening:

Bar-B-Q *Wendy Rene*
Cool Jerk *The Capitols*
One Thing Leads To Another *The Fixx*
Mellow Yellow *Donovan*
Happy Together *The Turtles*
Funky Cold Medina *Tone Loc*
All Along the Watchtower *Bob Dylan*
Take the "A" Train
    Duke Ellington & His Orchestra
Shake, Rattle and Roll *Big Joe Turner*
The Long Run *The Eagles*
You've Really Got a Hold On Me
    Smokey Robinson & The Miracles

Basil Garlic Mayonnaise

½ cup of your favorite mayonnaise

1 tablespoon dried parsley

Grilled garlic (see page 42)

2 teaspoons fresh basil, minced (to taste) **or 2 tablespoons dried basil**

Grill or roast a head of garlic (see page 42). In a food processor, with a mixer, or by hand blend the mayo, basil, and garlic until well mixed, about 30 seconds. Place in a sealed container in the refrigerator. This can be made ahead of time, but I will warn you that this spread will go fast; in my house it is always gone in a day or two.

5 minutes to make

This is a multi-use spread that can be a great flavor addition to sandwiches and vegetables. I like to use the basil mayo on sandwiches and wraps most of the time, and I will make a batch during the holidays to use for leftover turkey sandwiches. I top grilled asparagus, broccoli, and cauliflower with a dollop of this herbed mayonnaise on special occasions. A must for the Portobello Mushroom Sandwich (page 43).

Suggested Listening:

Statesboro Blues *The Allman Brothers*
Can't You Hear Me Knocking?
  The Rolling Stones
Stiff Upper Lip *AC/DC*
You Got It
  Count Basie & His Orchestra
Highway Star *Deep Purple*
Elegant Gypsy Suite *Al DiMeola*
When You Got a Good Friend
  Robert Johnson

Fiesta Seafood Cocktail Sauce

½ cup Smokin' Willie's Fiesta BBQ Sauce with Chipotle

3 tablespoons ketchup

2 tablespoons sweet pickle relish

½ teaspoon Worcestershire sauce

1 squeeze of fresh lemon juice, or ¼ teaspoon lemon juice

Here is another tough recipe! Mix all of the ingredients with a food processor, blender, immersion blender, or even by hand in a bowl.

Refrigerate and use as a dipping or cocktail sauce.

5 minutes to whip together

It was Saturday afternoon, and I had just finished the yard work and I didn't feel like going to the store to get something for dinner. Looking in the freezer for something to save me (the college football game was on soon), I found some frozen crab cakes but I did not have any seafood cocktail sauce. What I had was plenty of Smokin' Willie's Fiesta BBQ Sauce! Well, guess what happened—I concocted my own seafood sauce and now this is the only seafood sauce this family eats. This is a great dipping sauce and I use it to make lobster, crab, or shrimp cocktail. You will be blown away!

Suggested Listening:

On the Border *The Eagles*
Ventura Highway *America*
Toys In the Attic *Aerosmith*
Got My Mojo Working
 Muddy Waters
Rock Lobster *B-52's*
Dance To the Music
 Sly & The Family Stone
No More Tears *Ozzy Osborne*
Can't Stop the Rain *Los Lobos*
Boom, Boom Out Go the Lights
 Little Walter
The Lemon Song
 Jimmy Page & The Black Crowes

marinades, sauces, and butters

Grillin' Butters

1 stick unsalted butter, room temperature

1 teaspoon + Smokin' Willie's New Mexico Spice Rub or more to taste

1 teaspoon + parsley; use a little more if dried

¼ teaspoon Worcestershire sauce

¼ teaspoon water

Southwestern Grillin' Butter

Whip all of the ingredients in a bowl with an electric mixer. Refrigerate overnight for the flavors to develop, but you can use it right away if needed. This butter goes fast, so you might want to double this recipe. Store the butter in a Tupperware® butter dish that seals airtight in the refrigerator.

10 minutes mixing time

Chef Michael Acuna had talked to me about gourmet herb butters and convinced me that we should try making a Smokin' Willie's Grillin' Butter with herbs and spice rubs. Well, Michael was right as usual; the flavor was terrific! This butter is easy to make ahead of time. Just store it in your refrigerator. I use it for my grilled bread, corn on the cob, potatoes, vegetables, fish, shellfish, etc. A pat of Grillin' Butter on a steak just off the grill and you will think you are in one of those fancy steak houses!

Suggested Listening:

Whip It *Devo*
Whipping Post
  The Allman Brothers Band
Mellow Down Easy *Little Walker*
Baby Love
  Diana Ross & The Supremes
Yellow Ledbetter *Pearl Jam*
Paprika Plains *Joni Mitchell*
Silky Smooth *Larry Carlton*
Miss Judy's Farm *Faces*
Spanish Harlem *Aretha Franklin*
Country Comfort *Elton John*

Flavored Butters

1 stick unsalted butter at room temperature

1 teaspoon garlic powder (or use finely minced fresh garlic or roasted garlic)

¼ teaspoon onion powder

1 teaspoon dried parsley

1 teaspoon Smokin' Willie's New Mexico Spice Rub

¼ teaspoon Worcestershire sauce

¼ teaspoon water

Salt

Pepper

Garlic Butter

In a small mixing bowl place all of the ingredients and mix well with a food processor or hand-held cake mixer, 1½ to 2 minutes. Leave at room temperature if you are going to use right away or when used as a spread for bread. Refrigerate for up to 3 weeks. I usually double this recipe and use it up quickly.

Add parmesan and/or Romano cheese for a garlic cheese bread spread. Use Garlic Butter on baked potatoes and vegetables.

Options:
Smokin' Willie's Classic Rub
Fresh Cracked Pepper
Garlic (roasted, powder, or minced fresh)
Rosemary
Basil
Sage
Dill (for fish & veggies)
Lemon Juice instead of water (fish & veggies)
Most Herbs
Grated Parmesan and/or Romano Cheese

Remember that fresh herbs are stronger than dried herbs and to adjust the quantities for your taste buds. I put more of the ingredients in my butters, so when you are whipping up a batch, taste it and add more if you like.

10 minutes to make

You can make basic flavored butters and then experiment to match what you are cooking: dill when cooking veggies or to accompany seafood; rosemary and sage for poultry. You can use roasted or fresh garlic (which I think has a better flavor) or granulated or garlic salt in a pinch. Use more of the dried herbs than fresh; 1 teaspoon fresh is approximately 1 tablespoon dried when making these butters.

Suggested Listening:

Herbs and Roots *Joshua Redman*
Shake It Up *The Cars*
Look Sharp *Joe Jackson*
Rock Around the Clock
　Bill Haley & His Comets
Perpetual Change *Yes*
Let Me Try *Randy Travis*
Summer Wind *Frank Sinatra*
Wild *Seal*
The Main Thing *Roxy Music*
What You Need *INXS*
I Get a Kick Out Of You
　Clifford Brown & Max Roach

Grilled Vegetable Spread/Dip

1 cup grilled vegetables of your choice

Grilled garlic (see page 42)

Olive oil

2 tablespoons balsamic vinegar

Salt

Pepper

In a food processor or blender, place the vegetables, garlic, salt, pepper, balsamic vinegar, and a little olive oil and puree. Slowly add olive oil while mixing to spreadable consistency, not too thin. Use as a spread for sandwiches or use as a dip.

10 minutes prep
15 minutes grillin'
5 minutes to puree

Vegetables left over or grilled just for this purpose are used for this healthy vegetable spread/dip. This spread/dip is low in fat and has a taste that is amazing! Use your imagination and come up with different combos. I like to use peppers, onions, garlic, eggplant, mushrooms, and tomatoes. You can also use marinated artichoke hearts, marinated mushrooms, sun dried tomatoes, and roasted garlic. Use this spread on sandwiches, toasted cheese bread, and as a dip for chips and vegetables. Use a Mason jar to store any leftover spread in the refrigerator. For large groups or for picnics, use this spread to make rolled sandwiches using tortillas or Lavosh bread with the cheese and meat of your choice and lettuce and tomatoes wrapped in foil for easy transporting and eating.

Suggested Listening:

Take Me To the River *Talking Heads*
My Starter Won't Work *Lightnin' Slim*
You Better, You Bet *The Who*
Sweet Baby James *James Taylor*
Hungry Eyes *Merle Haggard*
Four Seasons *Vivaldi*
Yakety Yak *The Coasters*
Hey You *Pink Floyd*
Shake, Rattle and Roll *Big Joe Turner*
Tonight's the Night (Gonna Be Alright) *Rod Stewart*

Veggie Marinades

Simple & Easy Marinade

¼ cup extra virgin olive oil
½ tablespoon minced garlic
Salt
Pepper

Mix extra virgin olive oil, salt, and pepper and then lightly coat your veggies and grill. Use on the freshest of vegetables that you can get from the farmer's market to bring out the natural goodness!

Balsamic Vinegar & Olive Oil

This is my main squeeze for grilling vegetables—low in fat and simple to make. The variations are up to you and your palate. Flavored balsamic vinegars are great; I have been using a Fig Balsamic Vinegar lately and there are even more flavored olive oils. Use fresh or dried herbs to round off the flavor profile and you can even use this marinade as a salad dressing! I use this recipe with asparagus, eggplant, mushrooms, squash, and zucchini or a mixture of almost any vegetables. I also use this marinade for Portobello Mushroom Sandwiches (see page 43).

¼ cup balsamic vinegar (start off with regular, then experiment with flavored balsamic vinegars)
¼ cup extra virgin olive oil (herb-infused olive oils)
Basil (1 tablespoon dried or 10 to 12 leaves freshly chopped)
Salt
Pepper fresh from the mill

Place all of the ingredients but salt in a Mason jar or a container with a lid. Add a pinch of salt, cover, and shake vigorously for 15 to 20 seconds. Taste and add more salt if necessary. You can store this recipe, covered in the refrigerator, for up to two weeks (if it lasts that long).

Italian Salad Dressing

It does not get any easier than this: use your favorite Italian salad dressing to marinate vegetables. This is great for vegetable kabobs.

Shanghai Veggies

Use Smokin' Willie's Shanghai BBQ Sauce for an Asian fusion of flavor on mushrooms, asparagus, onions, peppers, and to make an amazing stir fry. You can use sesame seeds with this recipe for added flavor and texture.

5 minutes to prep

Marinating vegetables is a quick and simple way to enhance the flavors of the vegetables on the grill. Marinate softer vegetables like mushrooms and eggplant for up to 2 or 3 hours; any more than that and they can get soggy (but still good tasting). Firmer and larger veggies such as broccoli, onions, peppers, or tomatoes will not absorb much of the marinade until you start cooking on the grill. I use Mason jars, just like Grandma used to can fruits and vegetables, to use as a shaker to mix this marinade, and a gallon Ziploc® bag or Tupperware® to marinate the veggies. All of the ingredients in each recipe can be adjusted more or less to taste.

Suggested Listening:

More Than a Feeling *Boston*
Who Do You Love
  Ian Hunter with Mick Ronson
Caravan *Van Morrison*
The Romantic Warrior
  Return To Forever
Summer of Love *The B-52's*
25 or 6 to 4 *Chicago*
I Can't Quit You Baby
  Otis Rush
Today, Tomorrow, Forever
  Patsy Cline
Allison *Elvis Costello*
Got My Own Thing Now
  Squirrel Nut Zippers

desserts

Grilled Fruit

Pineapple

Apple

Pear

Peach

Apricot

Banana

Strawberry

Melon

Use your imagination

Halve and core/seed the fruit you are going to grill. Lightly coat the fruit with a nut oil. Grill the fruits first on the grill while the heat is high. You will have to stay at the grill because fruit will cook quickly, 5 to 15 minutes, depending on the heat of the grill and the thickness of the fruit. You want to sear the outside and get good color, and then remove from the grill. Let cool to room temperature uncovered (indoors) then cover and save for dessert.

You can also marinate the fruit in its own juices combined with 1 or 2 tablespoons of honey or brown sugar. Add cinnamon and/or nutmeg, or even a dash of Smokin' Willie's New Mexico Spice Rub for a little kick!

10 minute prep
10 to 15 minutes grilling time

Fruits are the most amazing food to grill, yet I do not hear people talk about grilling them very often. Healthy, quick, and great tasting, the flavors intensify over the heat of the grill. Try grilling some fruits and I will guarantee that you will start using fruits on the grill more and more. Start off with the firmer fruits like apples, pears, and pineapple and experiment your way to the more difficult fruits to grill like peaches. Bananas are also fun and easy. This is also a great way to get kids involved in cooking—and adding fruit to their diets!

Add a little coating of quality nut oil like macadamia, walnut, hazelnut, or pecan for great flavor and to seal in the juices. (With a little practice you can grill fruit at home to give you that restaurant/professional flavor.) Mix and match fruits, grill apples and pears at the same time, or make fruit skewers with softer fruits like strawberries and melons.

Suggested Listening:

Strange Fruit *Billie Holiday*
Sweetest Perfection *Depeche Mode*
Beautiful Mother Nature
   Ziggy Marley & The Melodymakers
I Love You For All Seasons *The Fuzz*
Don't Stop *Fleetwood Mac*
Happy Again *Chet Atkins*
Crimson & Clover
   Tommy James & The Shondells
Sing, Sing, Sing (With A Swing)
   Benny Goodman & His Orchestra
Sugar Magnolia *The Grateful Dead*
Gone, Gone, Gone *Miles Davis*
Summer Breeze *Seals & Crofts*

Bill's Grilled Bananas

3 firm bananas

1 tablespoon brown sugar

1 tablespoon melted butter or nut oil

1 tablespoon orange, lemon, or lime juice

¼ teaspoon ground cinnamon

Ground nutmeg

Peel the bananas then slice in half lengthwise, then cut in half again crosswise. Mix together melted butter, brown sugar, cinnamon, and juice and then coat the banana pieces. Grill directly over medium heat for just 2 or 3 minutes and flip over. Finish grilling for another 2 to 3 minutes then remove from the grill and cool to room temperature. Serve and enjoy!

Options:

Bananas by themselves or with other grilled fruits
Ice Cream Sundae: your favorite ice cream
Caramel and/or Chocolate Sauce
Peanuts
Almonds
Maraschino Cherries
Whipped Cream
Shredded Coconut
Candy Sprinkles
Imagine! Explore!

10 minutes prep
5 to 10 minutes grillin' time

Here is a great grilled fruit that is quick, easy, and fun. Use grilled bananas for a unique ice cream sundae or by themselves. Check out the list of options below for inspiration. You will want to use firm bananas that will hold up to grilling and not turn mushy. I usually use butter for this recipe, but you can also use a nut oil such as walnut, hazelnut, or macadamia. You will want to peel and slice the bananas just before grilling, and the orange, lemon, or lime juice will help keep the bananas from browning. For ice cream sundaes I grill the bananas early on the grill so they will be cool enough so as to not melt the ice cream.

Suggested Listening:

Love In the First Degree *Bananarama*
Every Day Is Like Sunday *Morrissey*
Kid Charlemagne *Steely Dan*
I've Got You Under My Skin
 Frank Sinatra
Summertime *Joe Sample*
Sweet Georgia Brown
 Django Reinhardt
No Strange Delight *Roxy Music*
Sugar Mama *Bonnie Raitt*
Food and Creative Love *Rusted Root*
One Hundred Ways *David Sanborn*

Grilled Pears

½ pear per person

Nut oil to lightly coat (macadamia, walnut, pecan, hazelnut, etc.)

Brown sugar

Wash, halve, and core pears; you can also peel them if you prefer. Place the pears in a dish and lightly coat them with nut oil. Sprinkle with brown sugar to taste. Let marinate for a little while, 15 to 20 minutes. Drain the pears and grill cut side down over direct medium heat for 8 to 10 minutes. Flip and finish grilling.

Toppings:

Add Cinnamon
Chopped nuts that match the oil you are using
Blue Cheese
Vinegar (balsamic, champagne-flavored)
Vanilla
"A La Mode" with Ice Cream
Whipped Cream
Chocolate Sauce
Caramel Sauce
Raisins
Be a child again and use your imagination—and let it go wild!

15 minutes prep
20 minutes marinating
15 to 20 minutes on the grill

Grilled fruit is a lot of fun, easy, and different. I find that firmer fruits are easier to grill when you first start out. I do not have a special story for this recipe, but I can tell you that everyone who tries grilled pears is surprised the first time and loves them!

Suggested Listening:

Take It Easy *The Eagles*
Brown Sugar *The Rolling Stones*
Sweet Dreams *Don Gibson*
So Beautiful *Boney James*
Lively Up Yourself *Bob Marley*
Our Lips Are Sealed *The Go Go's*
Swan Lake *Tchaikovsky*
Fruitful Days *Big Mountain*
I Don't Want To Wait *Paula Cole*
Betcha By Golly, Wow *The Stylistics*

Fruit Kabobs

Grapes for snacking while constructing kabobs

Strawberries

Bananas

Pineapple

Peaches

Nectarines

Apricots

Melon

Kiwi

Apples

Pears

Honey

Wooden skewers

Soak the wooden skewers in water for about a ½ hour prior to building the kabobs. Wash and clean all of the fruit. Cut into wedges (apricots, peaches, etc.) or cubes (melons). Alternate the fruit as you line the fruit on the skewers, putting strawberries on the ends as they do not need as much heat as the firmer fruit. Place completed fruit skewers on a medium high heat—you will have stay at the grill for this recipe because fruit grills quick. Turn the skewers after a few minutes until all sides are seared and move to indirect heat and brush honey lightly over the cooked kabobs and close the lid for a few minutes. Serve piping hot or cooled over a scoop of vanilla ice cream. The kids will have fun helping make this recipe! Clean the grill immediately after cooking to remove any honey that may have dripped on the grill surface.

Options:
Cinnamon
Nutmeg
Fresh Squeezed Lemon or Lime
Brown Sugar

10 minutes prep
5 to 10 minutes grillin' time

This is a fun and simple recipe for when the fresh summer fruit is ripe and sweet. The kids can make this one with Mom or Dad using the knife and supervising. I suggest that you have some grapes ready while you prepare this flavorful dish with the kids (that is, if you want any fruit left for the recipe, so you can snack while you build your kabobs!). Your imagination is the key to this recipe—that and Mother Nature. This recipe is great for the softer fruits like strawberries, peaches, and melons, but you can try any fruit combination that fits your fancy. I am going to list the main fruits that we have used in our home.

I try to shop for the ingredients the day before or the same day and pick firm but ripe fruit. If you are not sure about how to pick fruit that is ripe, talk to the produce person at the store and ask them to help you pick the best fruits and vegetables for your table. This recipe is great with or without cinnamon and nutmeg; there is something about the smell of cinnamon on the grill that brings back memories of Grandma's kitchen. I will always remember my grandmother's needlepoint that hung on her kitchen wall and read: "No matter where I serve my guests, they seem to like my kitchen best." At my house it would read: "No matter what I serve my guests, they seem to like my grillin' best!"

Suggested Listening:

Just Like Honey *Jesus And Mary Chain*
Sweet Dreams Are Made Of This *Eurythmics*
I Love You Honey *Patsy Cline*
Cool Jerk *The Capitols*
Didn't I (Blow Your Mind This Time) *The Delfonics*
Turn! Turn! Turn! *The Byrds*
Time Won't Let Me *The Outsiders*
Joy To the World *Three Dog Night*
A String of Pearls *Glenn Miller*
You Ain't Seen Nothing Yet *Bachman-Turner Overdrive*
Summertime *Miles Davis*

Nick's Stuffed Apples and Pears

2 apples, cored (Granny Smith, Golden Delicious, or baking apples)

2 pears, cored (Bartlett, Anjou, or Bosc)

3 tablespoons brown sugar

¼ cup graham cracker crumbs

½ teaspoon cinnamon

¼ cup raisins

¼ cup chopped walnuts or pecans

Grind down the graham crackers with a rolling pin into a lumpy flour consistency. Mix the graham crackers crumbs, brown sugar, cinnamon, raisins, and nuts in a bowl. Wash and core the apples and pears. Cut the bottom of the removed core about a ¼ inch thick to put back in the bottom of the apple and pear. Place fruit on a square of foil big enough to completely wrap the fruit. Fill the center of the fruit with filling (I pack to overflow, personally) and wrap and seal tight with foil. Place on grill over indirect heat.

I have had them cook in as fast as 20 minutes and take as long as 45 minutes, all depending on the heat. Grill starting with the bottom down and after 5 minutes turn on one side and rotate until cooked. To tell when the fruit is done, gently squeeze and it should feel like a baked potato, yielding but not mushy. Don't worry if you overcook the fruit; it will still taste great. Scout's honor!

Options:
Pecans
Dried Cranberries
Dried Fruit
Nutmeg
Lemon or Orange Zest
Peanuts
Cheese and Raisins

15 minutes prep
20 to 40 minutes on the grill

Here is a recipe from my youth. I was in the Boy Scouts and stuffed apples were the first fruit that I cooked over coals. We would prepare them ahead of time and cook them that night on the coals left over from cooking dinner. We would then eat them right from the foil they were wrapped in—messy dish, easy clean-up. You can slow cook this recipe putting the apples over indirect heat or you can even bake them in the oven. In the Boy Scouts we would leave the peel on, but sometimes I will peel the apples and pears (you have to cook them right away when you remove the peel).

Have the kids help you make them; they are easy to make and also a lot of fun. I remove the core with an apple corer and slice off the very bottom of the removed core and place it back in the bottom of the apple to keep the filling in. I like to use Granny Smith and Rome Beauty apples, but you can use any apple that you would bake with. I started using pears later on and discovered that they taste great! Use a ripe but firm pear like Bartlett, Anjou, or Bosc for the grill or it will be mushy when you go to eat it.

My son Nick was enjoying a stuffed apple when he stopped and said, "Dad, why don't you try graham cracker crumbs in the filling? It would taste like a pie crust." I do not know about the pie crust, but it sure did improve the taste! I now make my stuffing with cinnamon graham cracker crumbs and I experiment with the fillings—nuts, dried cranberries, lemon zest, or cheese and raisins. Every time I cook these stuffed fruits, the mouth-watering smell brings back memories of my youth and camping.

Suggested Listening:

Scrapple from the Apple *Charlie Parker*
Sticky Fingers *The Rolling Stones, the whole album*
Born In the U.S.A. *Bruce Springsteen*
I Heard It Through the Grapevine *Marvin Gaye*
Bust a Move *Young M.C.*
Sugar Foot Stomp *Fletcher Henderson & His Orchestra*
Do It (Till You're Satisfied) *B.T. Express*
Cool Jerk *The Capitols*
Wammer Jammer *J. Giles Band*
The Happy Song (Dum Dum) *Otis Redding*

BONUS RECIPE! GRAM'S CHOCOLATE-LOVERS CAKE

1 package Betty Crocker® Dark Chocolate Cake Mix

1/3 cup vegetable oil

3 eggs

Mom's Additions:

Cold coffee (replace the water with coffee called for in the recipe)

1/4 cup Best Foods® Mayonnaise

1½ cups Ghirardelli® Chocolate chips

Icing:

1 package Betty Crocker® Frosting Chocolate or Fudge

2 tablespoons bakers cocoa

Follow the directions on the box of the cake mix. Replace the water called for in the instructions with coffee. Avoid using instant coffee; Mom says it was awful. Add the mayonnaise and then the chocolate chips to the mixture and bake following the directions on the package.

Mix together the frosting and the cocoa powder using an electric mixer for about 2 minutes. Mom mixes the baker's cocoa with the ready-made frosting to give it a richer flavor. Sprinkle chocolate chips over the top of the cake.

Options: With Mom there are always options!
Nuts: Walnuts or Pecans
Butterscotch Chips

10 minutes to prep
30 to 35 minutes baking
10 minutes to frost the cake

If you or someone you know loves chocolate, then Mom has a cake for you! This recipe is so easy and tastes so rich and decadent no one will know that you made this cake from a box mix, plus a few of Mom's additions. Mom used to make a Devil's food cake from scratch, but it was difficult and time consuming. As I was growing up with my four brothers, it seems Mom just did not have the time to make her Devil's food cake as much as everyone wanted to eat it. Mom started tinkering with cake mixes and using her Devil's food cake recipe for inspiration to come up with this amazingly simple and tasty recipe. A good friend of hers told her she should try a little mayonnaise in the recipe and Mom has been using mayo ever since.

I copied this recipe exactly as Mom wrote it, even naming the brands that she uses. You can use whatever brand of ingredients that you like, but try making it Mom's way and see why this cake is one of her most requested desserts, especially by the pit crew. Hey guys, even if you are not very good at cooking you can make this cake and impress the love of your life. Nothing says "I love you" like chocolate.

Suggested Listening:

Cut the Cake *Average White Band*
Saturday Night Special *Lynyard Skynard*
Stay With Me *Rod Stewart*
Luck Be a Lady *Frank Sinatra*
Smooth Operator *Sade*
Every Little Thing She Does Is Magic *The Police*
Fix It In the Mix *Kevin Mahogany*
Back In Black *AC/DC*
Rock Steady *Aretha Franklin*
Barbados *Charlie Parker*

About the Author

Bill "Smokin Willie" Kelley *is the go-to guy if you want to know about grillin'. He's been tending the coals for over 3 decades and teaches classes, privately and in groups. He also does cooking demos at Whole Foods® Markets, Home Shows, and Fancy Food Shows—almost anyplace where people are enthusiastic about delicious food. A lifelong grillin' enthusiast, Bill made his passion his profession when he started Wild Bill's Foods in 2005. He has built a successful company on the foundation of his mom's spectacular barbecue sauce and his own love of grillin'. His thoughts, secrets, tips, and recipes are in his new signature book,* ***Smokin' Willie's Guide to Great Grillin'****. Bill lives in the Los Angeles area with Diana, his wife of 28 years, and their two sons, Matt & Nick, who wouldn't miss a family barbecue for anything.*

Please visit **www.smokinwillies.com** to find out where you can purchase Smokin' Willie's award-winning BBQ Sauces and BBQ spice rubs. Contact Smokin' Willie to speak to your group or teach grilling classes. Thank you!